BROOKLANDS

BB

**The Author
P J Wallace**

Born in 1896, P J Wallace worked as an engineer with many of the early manufacturers of motor cycles, aircraft, and aero engines. He entered the motor car industry in 1918, and in 1928 joined the company of D Napier & Son (later Napier Aero Engines). He retired in 1962 after long service with that company as chief test plant engineer

Editorial team

Editor-in-Chief, Ballantine Illustrated History Books
Barrie Pitt

Editorial Director
David Mason

Art Director
Sarah Kingham

Consultant Editor
Prince Marshall

Cover design: Michael Fry/Graham Bingham
Design: David Allen

First Printing: April, 1971

Printed in the United States of America

BALLANTINE BOOKS, INC.
101 Fifth Avenue, New York, N.Y. 10003
An Intext Publisher

Contents

Photographs and illustrations for this book have been selected from the following archives: Old Motor Magazine, Ronald Barker, Angus Clark, The Autocar, Montagu Motor Museum, T A S O Mathieson, Radio Times Hulton Picture Library, The Motorcycle, William Boddy, Flight Magazine, N W Lewis

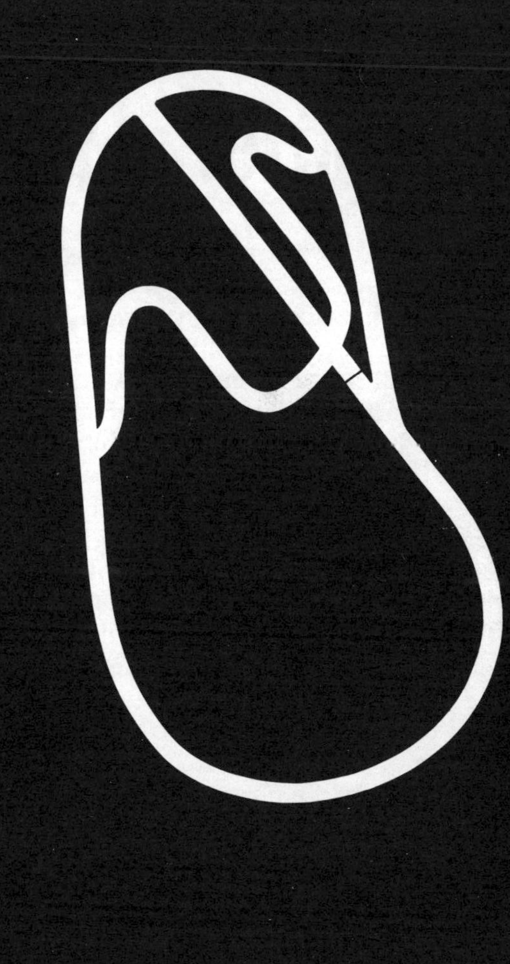

Memories of pioneer days

Looking back to my student days, it seems a long time ago I bought my first racing car – a black Riley Nine 'Brooklands' model – and entered and ran it without distinction in the Autumn meeting of the Brooklands Automobile Racing Club in 1931. But I was attracted by the sport, and above all by the atmosphere at this track, and managed the next year to find a faster car, a 2 litre Bugatti, and then later a 2½ litre Maserati, which I used mainly on the Mountain circuit. For the next few years, until I gave up racing for a more serious preoccupation with flying, I had many happy times, mainly on this Mountain circuit, where I managed to break a record or two.

Brooklands had a charm of its own. It had variety, with several meetings a year, many consisting of several short races, others with longer races, sometimes of an international character. It had a country club atmosphere – everyone knew everyone else! It catered for all pockets, from those lucky enough to have a Maserati or a 3.3 Bugatti to the young enthusiast who could scrape up enough to buy an Ulster Austin or an Anzani Frazer-Nash. Because many races were handicaps, everyone had a chance – at least once until 'Ebby' the handicapper got wise to you. Exciting to the spectator and the competitor alike was the appearance of the Brooklands monsters, the Chitty Chitty Bang Bang or V12 Delages which smoked in the paddock and thundered around the track at the top of the banking.

But these days are in the past. In 1939 we were at the limit of safety on the 'banked' circuit and indeed on the Campbell circuit. By 1945 the track surface, always bad, had deteriorated beyond acceptable limits, and car design had progressed to the point where track racing on aerodrome type circuits offered much more scope for spectacle, and also indeed to the designer to develop suspension systems, brakes and tyres. So after the war it was decided not to re-open the track – a wise decision, I would say. While clearly in the early days Brooklands was of tremendous importance to motor manufacturers, especially to the makers of accessories, tyres, fuel, carburettors and so on, since nowhere else could they drive their cars at continuous speed; as time went on and Continental contests became more popular, the track grew less important. Today the makers prefer the privacy of their own test tracks. Unfortunately, it is the amateur who has lost out; at Brooklands he could spend all day in peace tuning his car, trying different jets and plugs, and speed as much as he liked. Today there is nowhere for him to go except an empty motorway on a Sunday morning and then, in Britain at least, he must keep to 70 mph.

However regrettable to have to admit it, it is pure sentiment to believe that motor racing would have benefited with the re-opening of the track, although I confess to wishing I could once again be in the paddock before a race or at the start of a Mountain Handicap with 'Ebby' starting off a single seat Austin, a pair of supercharged MGs, ERAs, Maseratis, Bugattis . . . it would be idle to suggest that events like this with modern cars would attract the public, even if the traffic congestion and noise problems in the Weybridge area could be tolerated.

But if we cannot turn the clock back and have Brooklands again, we can at least read about it in this splendidly vivid book and gaze at the illustrations, evoking a nostalgia from having been there for some of us, and from not having been there in others!

Whitney Straight

IMPROVING THE BREED

Brooklands is a name which at different times has meant different things to different people. To some it was just two or three square miles of grassland, roughly oval in shape and surrounded on its three-mile perimeter by a ribbon of concrete a hundred feet wide. Set adjacent to an embankment of the old London and South-Western Railway, about twenty miles from Waterloo Station, it was something to look out for (yet easily missed) from the window of an express train speeding on its way between London and Southampton. To others it was a place where lunatics endangered their lives in racing cars or motor-cycles, or sought suicide in primitive aeroplanes constructed of wood, piano wire and fabric. To many of the local residents it was just a public nuisance, a source of penetrating noise accompanied by an offensive odour of burnt oil. To one small and specialised profession it was a mere sewage farm located in unusual surroundings. All these people, whatever their particular prejudice or point of view, shared one thing in common – they knew very little about Brooklands.

Brooklands was not just a place on the map, or one to be defined by the activities of its habitués; rather it was an institution, almost a way of life, to be savoured and understood only by the initiated. To those who came to watch, no less than those more actively involved, the roar and crackle of engine-exhaust was music in the ear and the odour of burnt oil a source of spiritual refreshment. Even the sewage farm came to acquire a legendary character unique in the annals of public sanitation.

It is unlikely that any ideas of this sort were present in the minds of those pioneers who conceived and engineered the great motor racing track, the first of its kind in the world. On the contrary, they were concerned with very practical ends – the provision of a track where motor-cars could be driven continuously, and in comparative safety, at maximum speed, thus enabling manufacturers to develop the performance, safety and reliability of engine and chassis to a degree otherwise impossible to attain. Realising that on this basis alone the venture might not produce an adequate return

on invested capital, they further proposed to organise from time to time race-meetings to which the general public would be admitted according to a scale of charges.

The first of these objectives was achieved with complete success; over a period of thirty-two years, from 1907 to 1939, the track was in constant use by cars running at speeds extending to well beyond 100mph. As could scarcely be avoided, accidents occurred from time to time although few of them were fatal. On the other hand, as a place of public resort and entertainment Brooklands never really made the grade. Attendance at many meetings could be numbered in hundreds rather than the thousands which had been expected. It is true that on special occasions the gate might exceed thirteen or fourteen thousand, but what were these in so vast an amphitheatre?

However, the importance of Brooklands is not to be measured in terms of numbers; neither is its life to be defined merely as a succession of race meetings. Such events were only occasional – at the most two or three a month during the season. Whatever may have been in the minds of the promoters, the effective purpose of these meetings did not lie in gate-money. What they provided was a constant stimulus to numbers of men dedicated to the cause of speed. These men were to be seen, every day of the week, striving in their worksheds to extract a few more mph from their machines or out on the track discovering whether they had been successful. It was largely through their striving that motor-vehicles were to be so vastly improved.

In respect of the early years, it would be more accurate to say that by these means the performance of the petrol engine was to be so greatly accelerated; for motor-cars comprise more than their engines. Nowhere else in the world (except on the test-bench, and that has its own limitations) was it possible for engines to develop their full power for hours at a time without interruption. Only by these long spells of sustained maximum

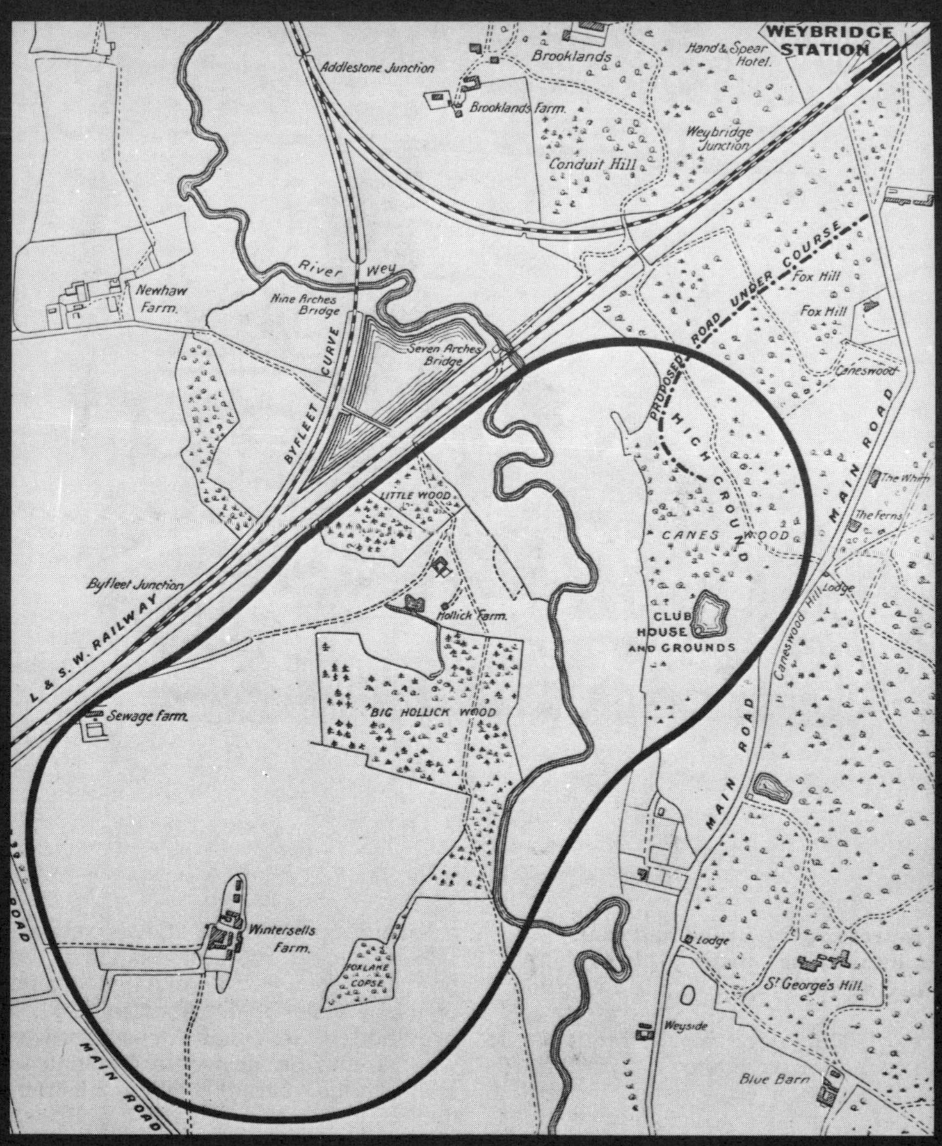

power could the engine become so 'soaked' with heat as to expose every facet of its design and construction to the ultimate test. These same conditions were equally valuable in the ultimate evolution of the modern pneumatic tyre.

H F Locke King, the prime instigator of Brooklands and owner of the land on which the track was built

The original proposal of 1906 showing environs of Brooklands

While track-racing made its contribution in other directions, such as steering, suspension, transmission and brakes, only the hard braking and violent accelerations necessary on a sinuous and undulating course could prove really searching. Some twenty

Improving the Breed had many connotations – testing this 40/45hp ABC aero engine on a wind waggon

years later steps would be taken to introduce a modicum of such hazards at Brooklands. It is rather ironical to reflect that these additions were adopted not out of any direct concern for 'improvement of the breed' but in a belated endeavour to reattract a public who had found the high-speed procession of cars on the original circuit too boring to warrant their regular attendance.

The original decision to embark upon the construction of Brooklands, regarded strictly as a financial venture, would seem a notable example of judgement based on hope rather than calculated probability. It was reasonable to expect good attendance at the opening meetings if only on account of the novelty of the spectacle to be provided; the vital question was whether the public would continue to come. In the year 1906 when construction of the track began, the British public as a whole was by no means enamoured of the motor-car. The popular image, deriving from early attempts at the horseless carriage, was a rather nasty-smelling, noisy and vibrating contraption perpetually liable to breakdown. The great majority of people were quite unaware of the considerable progress which had been made since then; moreover, there had been little opportunity to learn. Comparatively few people had experienced a ride in a car and these had necessarily been members of the more affluent classes; the motor-bus and the motor char-à-banc (the precursor of the motor-coach) were still in their infancy.

Even less was known of motor-racing; and what information there was inspired horror rather than envy. Forbidden on the public highways of Great Britain, all the big races had taken place on the continent. Newspaper reports of these events had tended towards the sensational with undue emphasis on fatalities. This kind of picture offered but slight attraction to a people whose national sports and recreations were cricket, football and horse-racing. Stories of the chaos and tragedy attendant upon the Paris-Madrid race of 1903, when a total of 275 assorted vehicles had charged at speeds of anything up to 60 or 70mph along unfenced roads lined by three million people subject to no effective marshalling, had left an indelible impression. In the face of such a situation, public reaction to Brooklands inevitably remained a matter for speculation.

From a strictly technical point of view, expectations were much more securely based; a number of men who had gained distinction in motor-racing abroad and were influential in the motor industry had already pledged their support. Most notable among

. . . or fuel consumption and endurance for an American car

. . . or George Eyston demonstrating his faith in the oil engine

them was S F Edge who held the sole concession for sale of the famous Napier cars; together with H F Locke King, the owner of the land on which the track was to be built, who shared primary responsibility for inspiration of the scheme. In principle, this scheme was simple enough – a closed circuit around which cars could travel in reasonable safety at speeds around 100mph and wide enough to permit them to overtake freely and safely. Colonel Holden RE was appointed to design the course and to supervise the civil engineering.

Excepting some criticism attaching to the finished concrete surface, a matter which will be discussed in due course, all this engineering may be said to have been carried out to the highest standards. If public support at race-meetings, and with it the takings at the gate, proved a source of disappointment the same cannot be said of the technical results. The practicability of 120mph was soon to be demonstrated although the ride was found to be much rougher than had been hoped. As time progressed, there appeared ample evidence of 'improvement of the breed'. Monster cars with pistons larger than top-hats were steadily superceded by more scientifically designed vehicles of progressively smaller cylinder capacity, the sequence occasionally interrupted by improvised adaptations of high-power aero engines. At the beginning, the

. . . or the 24–hour endurance run for a new marque of AEC bus

AEC "REGENT
MT 2114

The ugly duckling that became the swan – one of A V Roe's early efforts

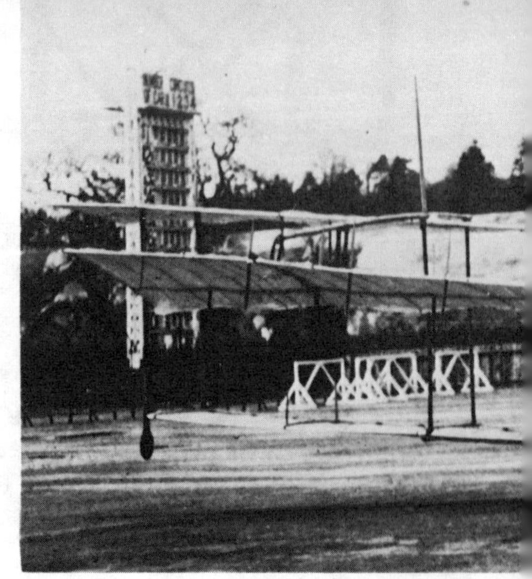

monstrous FIATs of eighteen (or even twenty-eight) litres and capable of something in the 120s; at the end, the diminutive Austin Seven with pistons the size of egg-cups yet lapping at more than 100mph. This was unmistakably 'improving the breed'.

To that extent the founders may safely be credited with foresight of the pattern of events which would flow from their enterprise. What they could not possibly foresee was the vital contribution which Brooklands was to make in spheres far removed from motor-racing. In the year 1907, the flights of the Wright brothers were still regarded with deep scepticism; only

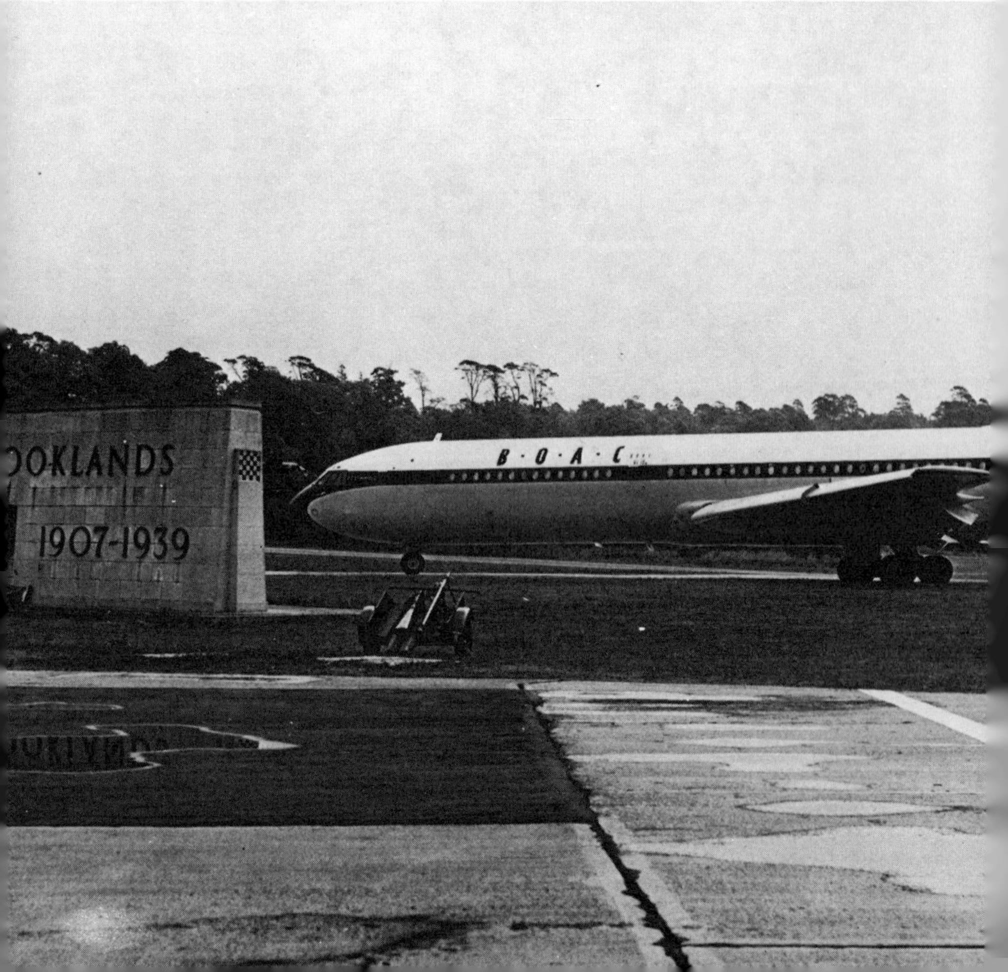

a tiny minority believed in the bare possibility of mechanical flight. Who, then, could foresee that within six years of its opening Brooklands would attract a record gate, not to watch racing-cars hurtling round the concrete but to see a pilot, high in the sky, looping-the-loop in an aeroplane? That the great expanse of concrete would eventually fall into ruin and decay, its pride of place usurped by the flat land (sewage-farm included) contained within its perimeter, was a contingency beyond conception.

Within three months of opening-day, appeared the lone shed of a solitary would-be aviator. A year or two later would come the more commodious hangers of the flying-schools and a few pioneer makers of aircraft. Here, the line of progress would curve in an opposite direction to that which would mark the racing-car; it would begin with a minature and end with a giant. At first a primitive aeroplane weighing (with pilot) 450lbs became – on 8th June 1908 – the first plane to fly in England; meanwhile, the monster cars roared their way round the track. In 1936, while the Austin egg-cups were

and the swan VC 10 rolled onto the track, for a press viewing

Brooklands in decline

getting into their stride, there took off from Brooklands the first Vicker's 'Wellington' weighing some twenty tons and able to fly at 250mph. On the 29th June 1962, long after the track had fallen into decay, there followed the take-off of the first Vicker's 'VC 10' weighing 140 tons and able to cruise at nearly 600mph.

Such was the enormous diversity of machines which showed their paces at Brooklands; yet the list is not complete. On no account must one overlook the racing motor-cycles whose riders contributed as much as any to the spirit of the place; and it is in terms of the spirit no less than material achievement that the essence of Brooklands is to be understood. The machines were remarkable enough but the men who designed, tuned and raced (or flew) them were even more remarkable and infinitely more important. Their dedication to the cause of speed was to exert a far-reaching influence on the development of the motor-car and to make an irreplaceable contribution to aviation and, especially, the evolution of the aero-engine. Through its flying schools, it was to provide a substantial proportion of those pilots who would constitute the original nucleus of the Royal Flying Corps and thus the Royal Air Force. Without Brooklands the pattern of the history of motorised vehicles would have taken a different shape.

Enthusiasts, their better judgement temporarily obscured by nostalgia, plead that Brooklands should be 'brought back'. If by the phrase 'brought back' they mean the restoration of the concrete track to its original use, the idea is at least conceivable, even though the practical difficulties might be immense; but that would not be the same thing as 'bringing back Brooklands'. As an institution and a way of life it can never be brought back; for it was the product of an age and a generation which have passed, never to return.

AN ASTONISHING ACHIEVEMENT

The site chosen for the projected motor-course lay in close proximity to the pleasant town of Weybridge and was set in the type of wooded heathland characteristic of that part of Surrey. The area was of elongated shape whose length of little more than a mile was roughly twice the width at the mid-point, the two long sides being convergent. While the greater part was flat, there occurred towards the north-east corner a very substantial hillock. The general topography was such as to afford a number of choices in determining the configuration of the circuit. The simplest form would clearly have been a true circle such as had been employed in the few small cycle race-tracks already in existence, but this was open to serious objections. In addition to wasting half the available area, the maximum diameter would have been limited to about 5/8 of a mile; this would have meant that a car when travelling at 120mph completed a circuit every fifty-three seconds and the spectacle would have been so appallingly boring to everybody concerned as to render the idea rather ridiculous.

If the fullest use was to be made of the available space the question arose as to what should be done with the hillock. Three alternatives were possible; to by-pass it on the inside, to carry the track over the top or, as was in fact decided, to carve a way through the lower part of the outer slope. Choice of the second alternative would certainly have provided a thrilling spectacle at race-meetings; its rejection is the surest evidence that Brooklands was never planned with public entertainment as the primary objective.

No matter what configuration be given to a closed circuit, it is only too obvious that portions of it must consist of curves; and that vehicles travelling around these curves will be subjected to centrifugal force. This force will be proportional to the square of the speed and inversely proportional to the radius of curvature. The centrifugal force must be resisted by the frictional adhesion between tyre and track, otherwise the car will slide (side-slip) outwards from the curve. If the height of the centre of gravity of the vehicle be sufficiently high in relation to the track-width between the wheels then the vehicle

The track seen from the air in its original guise and before the building of the Campbell straight

will capsize. Both of these untoward events may be averted by inclining (banking) the surface of the track upwards towards the outside of the curve. This expedient is widely adopted on railways where it is known as super-elevation.

It will be evident that for every combination of curvature and banking in respect of their radius and inclination, there will be one speed (and one only) at which the vehicle will be completely free of any tendency either to side-slip or overturn. This means that on a properly designed race-track, where the steepness of the banking increases progressively towards the outside edge, there will exist a line along which the car may be driven at any given speed within the track's capacity without applying any force to the steering-wheel; the position of this line depending upon the speed. Theoretically, with a perfectly smooth track-surface the car will steer itself.

It is important to remember that so far as the centrifugal force is not balanced by the inclination of the banking a number of unpleasant things can happen. Any unbalanced side-thrust from the centrifugal force (or from any other source for that matter) will put a side-load on the tyre and tend to pull it out of the well in the wheel-rim. According to the geometry of the steering layout – that is to say according to whether the point of contact between front wheel and track lies ahead of, abaft of, or coincident with, the axis about which the wheel is turned for steering purposes, there will occur a torque, or turning force, on the steering wheel which must be resisted by the driver. According to the magnitude of this displacement, and all the other conditions, this torque can reach levels that can tax even the most powerful drivers.

In the same way, if a car should deliberately be driven below the 'natural' position on the banking it will only be done by the driver exerting the appropriate force in the opposite direction. As has already been mentioned, the preceeding discourse assumes that the track surface is perfectly

smooth. So long as that be the case, the driver will readily 'feel' when his car is travelling along the line appropriate to his speed; any slight departure will be open to easy and immediate correction. If, on the other hand (and as so often happened) the car should proceed from one bump to the next, with one or more of the wheels high in the air, the most strenuous efforts will be necessary if the car is to be kept on the track at all and prevented from flying over the top of the banking.

When all the various factors are taken into account – the topography of the site, the various hazards outlined above and the necessity of ensuring the highest degree of safety – there can be no doubt that Colonel Holden produced a masterly piece of work; it is ever to be regretted that the physical execution of his plans did not attain quite so high a standard: the 'perfectly smooth' surface, whether it was ever attainable or not, was never achieved. The matter has given rise to arguments which are never likely to be resolved. One school of thought has always maintained that the workmanship was of a quality entirely comparable with the design and that the surface was irredeemably damaged by the pounding received from S F Edge's Napier cars in the course of their onslaught on the twenty-four hour record a few days before the first race-meeting was held. The theory is certainly worth further examination.

Despite the fact that concrete of one form or another had been in use since time immemorial, and Portland cement for more than a century, much had yet to be learned regarding techniques best adapted to particular circumstances. The laying of a wafer (for that is what a six-inch thickness amounted to) over so vast a continuous surface was without precedent, equally unprecedented was the nature of the load to be borne on it. It is, in fact, the entire novelty of the scheme which renders so

S F Edge; the first man to put Brooklands 'on the map'

inexplicable the omission to employ steel reinforcement together with some form of expansion joint between adjacent sections. Of equal importance is the time factor. The transformation of wooded country into a finished racing-track in a period of little more than nine months may well have left some of the concrete surface insufficient time to harden and mature.

Even more to the point, much of the underlying soil had perforce to be dug to a deeper level or built up to a higher one with inadequate time for consolidation before the concrete was laid. The intervening layer of sand could do nothing to mitigate the subsidence of soil beneath it. A subsidence having once occurred, it was likely to remain a permanent blemish; for once the track had come into commission even less time was likely to be available for consolidation of the added material. Some of the resultant bumps and hollows were soon to become notorious and to remain so for the life of the track. Far more numerous were the ruts and shallow water channels which in course of time developed along the lines where one slab of concrete butted against its neighbours; disconcerting enough to car-drivers, they could be lethal to the racing motor-cyclist.

The configuration finally chosen for the course was the longest continuous circuit which could be accommodated without any substantial re-entrant curves. By suitable excavation through the outer slope of the hillock (henceforward to be known as the 'Members' Hill') there was obtained a natural banking (twenty-nine feet high) as required for the sharpest curve (1,000-foot radius) of the course. This 'Members' Banking' ended in a downward incline (one in twenty-five along the path of travel) to join the straight and level stretch (5/8 of a mile long and known as the 'Railway Straight') which ran parallel and adjacent to the main railway line. This straight terminated in the wide sweep (1,550-foot radius) of the Byfleet Banking (twenty-two feet high), its name borrowed from the

Cross sectional view of the course as originally planned.

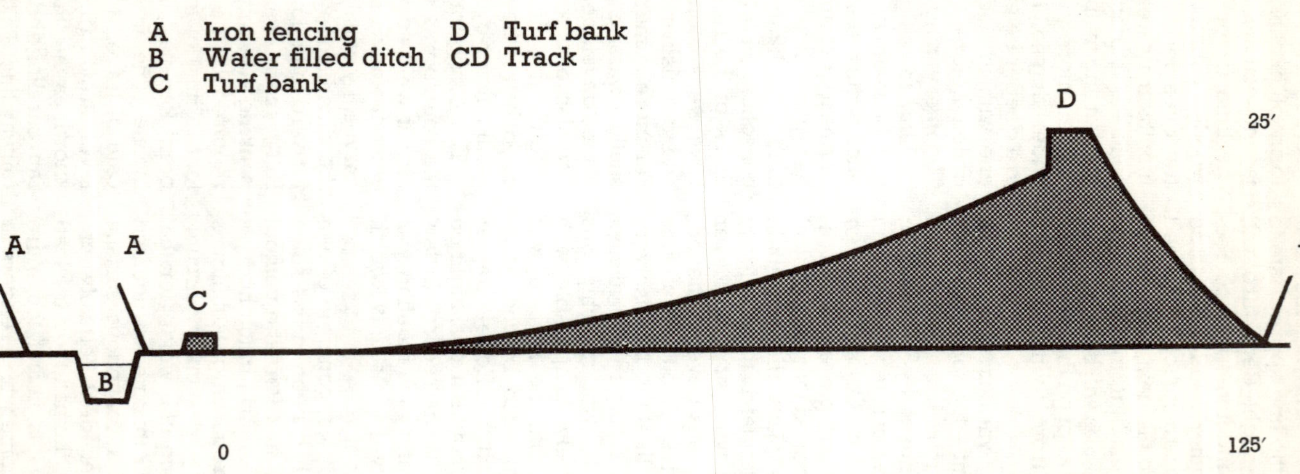

It should be noted that the parapet indicated at 'D' occurred only over the short length which bridged the river Wey

then village which lay on the other side. This curve extended through more than a semi-circle to join the last section, close enough to a straight line to need no banking, and rose through an upward gradient of one in thirty to rejoin the Members' Banking. The entire circuit was almost $2\frac{3}{4}$ miles in length and of this a total of two miles was level.

Roughly mid-way along this shorter straight and at a point later to be known as the 'Fork', a chordal section branched off to the left. This 'Finishing Straight' cut directly across to rejoin the main circuit in a sharp right-angled junction situated towards the end of the Members' Banking. On its way it skirted the foot of the inner slope of the Members' Hill, thus in effect turning this hill into an 'island'. Facing the hill and on the other side of the Finishing Straight was the 'Paddock', a fenced enclosure at the centre of which stood the club building and administrative offices. Excepting the occasions of car race-meetings, when other arrangements were provided for the general public, normal entry to the track was through the Paddock which was reached by a roadway which passed through a tunnel under the Members' Banking.

Advantage was taken of the steep inner slope of the hillock to construct a concrete-surfaced 'Test Hill'. Leading out of the finishing straight, this was arranged in a series of short straight sections which became progressively steeper towards the top of the hill; it was only wide enough to take one car at a time. While quite useful in the early days when hill-climbing speeds were low, Test Hill later came to be much neglected; the quick and sharp turn in the communicating roadway at the top rendered record attempts distinctly hazardous. Further on, this roadway continued by means of a narrow bridge over and beyond the high Members' Banking and finally joined the entrance road leading to the Paddock.

If travelled in the reverse direction – a practice much favoured by motor-cyclist members – it afforded a magnificent view embracing the whole of Brooklands except for the short section hidden behind the hill. It was at the brow of the hill that the olfactory nerves would grow tense to the subtle and distinctive odour of 'Wakefield's Castrol R' or perhaps, if an old box-kite happened to be flying around, the equally stimulating smell of burnt castor oil from its rotary Gnome engine. The combination of smell and vision produced within the initiate an overpowering urge to get cracking round the circuit at the earliest possible moment. It would be most unfortunate if anybody should happen to be coming up the Test Hill!

However, this is looking as yet into the future; between the stages of design and use, the track had somehow to be built. In the light of present-day techniques, the methods of construction bordered upon the primitive. It now seems almost incredible that men unaided by modern machinery and dependent upon unknown numbers of horses and carts should have completed this enormous task in so short a time as nine months; still more so that completion date should be so near to what had been specified long in advance. Statements have varied as to the total labour-force employed on the job, one writer having put it as high as 2,000. On the other hand Locke King, in the course of his speech at the inaugural lunch, referred to 700 men having worked through the winter. Of course, it is by no means unusual on these occasions for principals to be inadequately briefed on points of detail; whether the number was one or the other makes no difference, the work of construction was an astonishing achievement.

The credit due to horses and men is in no way diminished by the fact that several miles of temporary railroad were laid communicating with the London and South-Western Railway main-line for delivery of the enormous quantities of material required. This detail serves to emphasize resemblance

between the methods of constructing Brooklands racecourse and the laying-out of a great network of railways during the previous century. Both were sullied by the appalling conditions in which the labourers were forced to live. It could hardly be said to be a case of wilful inhumanity on the part of employers; they saw it as the way things had always been done before and lacked the imagination to do anything better. Social welfare was not a top priority in 1906.

Hordes of men working, eating, drinking and sleeping on the site, housed in improvised hovels of their own building out of any materials which happened to lie at hand; the local residents half-terrorised by the drunkenness, fighting and general rowdyism commonplace between shifts: it is difficult to relate such a picture to the magnificent result. There would not appear to have occurred the kind of labour dispute which has since become familiar. In fact, such was the general confidence in completion of the work to the prearranged schedule that

These were the means by which most of the earth was moved

This picture will convey some idea of the vast masses of earth which were moved during the work of construction

the newly-formed Brooklands Automobile Racing Club (BARC), as early as December 1906, was inviting entries for an opening race-meeting to be held ('if possible') during the coming May. At much about the same time, S F Edge announced his intention of attempting a new twenty-four record as soon as the track should become ready for use.

These announcements of arrangements stimulated interest in quarters where so far it had not been particularly apparent – the editorial and correspondence pages of the motoring press. It cannot be said that the general tone of opinion expressed was either entirely favourable or enthusiastic. Editorials deplored the lack of interest on the part of industry and expressed strong doubt regarding the prospects of the venture achieving financial success; correspondents were not convinced that track-racing could lead to better motor-cars, contending that running conditions would be very different from those experienced by

the private motorist. Editors did less than they might have done to counter the point of view. While asserting that Brooklands would be effective in 'improving the breed', little explanation was offered in support; one editor in particular was more concerned with the manner in which racing would be conducted.

Observing that financial return must depend upon the gate, he was at pains to point out that public support would depend upon the races being run 'straight' and free from all shady practices; in this connection doubts were expressed concerning the wisdom of introducing bookmakers and betting. This cautionary attitude was doubtless inspired by recollections of abuses which had been known elsewhere. As events turned out, bookmakers commenced operations at the very first meeting and remained for the years that followed without any of the unpleasantness which had been feared. These men were to acquire a new humility imposed by baffling difficulties in estimating form; a favoured horse might suffer fits of temperament, it could not be fitted with a new camshaft overnight.

The same editorial further advocated that manufacturers should not exploit unduly the advertising potential of racing successes. The reasons for this advice are hard to understand, for what more powerful incentive could induce industry to engage in so costly a business as motor-racing? In point of fact, advertising was to become the very life-blood of motor-racing in one form or another and to provide not only an incentive but also the financial resources without which many could never otherwise have afforded to compete.

Inevitably, there was a general disposition to think in terms of the organisation and practices of horse-racing, the sport of kings and 'gentlemen'. Cars would be entered by gentlemen and driven by jockeys who would be

Colonel Holden

identified by their masters' colours. Of course, people should have known better but they did not, they had yet to learn. Accordingly, it is somewhat surprising to find that the prospectus for the opening race-meeting, issued during the previous December, should have included a cut-price offer. Entry fees ranging from £20 to £150 would be reduced to £10 and £50 if the money was received by 15th January. It is not known to what extent this special offer was patronised. It was further stated that prize-money to the amount of £4,500 would be distributed among the successful competitors.

The period of waiting for the racecourse to be completed would not appear to have been marked by that degree of anticipation or depth of technical speculation such as would accompany any enterprise of comparable magnitude and novelty today. It is true that, in an unguarded moment, one editor visualised cars travelling at over 100mph 'within two feet of the inner edge'. Even more intriguing was the publicising of an incident suggesting that racing-drivers did not necessarily exclude their professional capacity for ruthless determination from their private lives. It related how S F Edge, driving home from the South Coast one bitterly cold night, was grievously insulted by some callow youth during a brief stop. Seizing the miscreant by the scruff of the neck, Edge forced him into the car and took him ten miles along the road; here he set him down, minus his trousers, to make his own way back. Obviously, these record-breakers were not men to be trifled with!

Seemingly quite out of character with the purposes for which Brooklands was being built, much attention was devoted to preparations for a 'Dust Trial' proposed to be held soon after the track should come into commission. In those days of untarred roads, dust was the curse of motoring to both motorist and any other user of the roads. It was, presumably, the impossibility of finding a stretch of dust-free

Last phase of construction on the Members' Hill

highway which determined the selected venue. Not unreasonably, it was considered that both the shape of the vehicle and the measurement of ground clearance might be major factors affecting the degree of the nuisance and that controlled experiments might open the way to substantial improvement. By way of anticipation, it must be recorded that the tests were duly held but failed to provide any hopeful solution to the problem.

Whatever may have been the general display of indifference towards the fast-approaching opening day, there was one quarter where feverish preparations were in progress. S F Edge, supported by the engineering resources of the Napier company, strove day and night to exploit an unrivalled opportunity.

Wide-angle view from the Members' Hill soon after opening-day

MELTING POT OF PROGRESS

The official opening of Brooklands took place on 17th June 1907. The inaugural lunch and its speeches were followed by what was intended to be a formal procession of cars round the circuit, instructions being issued to the effect that there should be no overtaking. This was asking rather a lot from a gathering of enthusiasts suddenly let loose in a variety of cars ranging from 10 to 90hp on a new course reputedly designed for safe motoring at speeds in excess of 100mph. Despite the measure of indiscipline only to be expected under the circumstances, no serious accident occurred and a good time was had by all.

Serious business was to begin some eleven days later when S F Edge and his supporting team would set out on their historic drive which would establish or break a whole sheaf of world speed records. As may already have been surmised, Edge was not a man accustomed to doing things by halves; above all, he was a master of publicity. There was to be no playing about with flying miles or kilometres, records which might easily pass unnoticed; if

necessary they could come later. What was needed to put Brooklands and, incidentally, Napier cars well and truly on the map was something which would make a real impact upon the imagination of the public. What could be better for this purpose than twenty-four hours continuously at the wheel, high on the banking at speeds faster than an express train?

A well-known racing cyclist at twenty, he later became a branch manager of the Dunlop Tyre Company, a sphere of activity bound to bring him into closest contact with early motor-cars and their pioneering manufacturers. He was among the first, if not in fact *the* first, to forsee the immense possibilities which lay ahead. Although not an engineer he soon grasped the fundamentals through personal experience of the vagaries of a 6hp Panhard Levassor which he had purchased. Later, he chanced to meet Montague Napier who, in a works which had been founded by his grandfather, was applying himself to the problems of designing and making a better type of motor car than had so far been produced.

The conjunction of these two remarkable men was to yield equally remarkable results. Having entered into an exclusive undertaking to sell all the cars which Napier could make, Edge proceeded to publicise their undoubted merits as widely as possible. He was quick to see that racing and other forms of competition would best suit his purpose. In 1901, he drove a Napier car in the second Gordon Bennett race in France but was compelled to retire owing to clutch trouble. The following year he had better luck and won the race, to the astonishment and chagrin of the French who had considered themselves unbeatable.

It would be out of context to relate all the detail of Edge's early motoring career; let it suffice that by the time the new track was opened he had become a notable if not famous personality. Meanwhile, Napier had been devoting engineering ability of the highest order towards the evolution of what would later be advertised as 'The Best Car in the World'. As had been the case with the great engineers who had preceeded him, Montague Napier attracted to his service young men of corresponding quality, totally dedicated to his cause and prepared to give of their utmost. Such were the men who were to support S F Edge in the approaching event. One of them in particular, H C Tryon, was in course of time to exemplify those many links which can be traced from the early days of Brooklands through improvement of the breed of motor-car to the ultimate perfection of the modern aero-engine.

It has been so often forgotten that when, on 28th June 1907, Edge began his assault on the twenty-four hour record he did not compete alone; two other 60hp Napier cars belonging to Edge accompanied his own and all three achieved substantially the same performance. His distinction was to be the only driver who completed the full distance without relief, the other two cars being driven alternately by

Above: S F Edge with mechanic in the 90hp Napier 'Samson'. Right: Score card for the 24 hour record. Below: Sir George Abercromby's 40hp Napier, similar in many respects (except hp) to those which established the 24 hour record a few months earlier

... AT ...
BROOKLANDS TRACK,
WEYBRIDGE,

STARTING at 6 p.m., JUNE, 28th, 1907,

Mr. S. F. EDGE will attempt to beat

the existing

24 Hours World's Motor Track Record

on a

SIX CYLINDER NAPIER CAR.

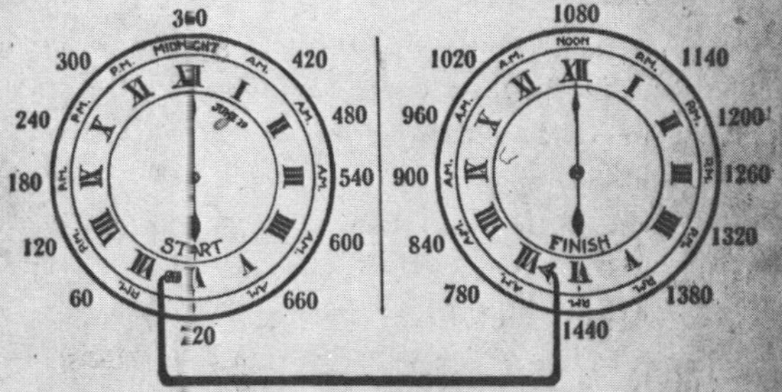

This represents the total miles which must be accomplished hourly to keep up 60 miles per hour.

Comparisons of previous 24 hours distances with present attempts.

* Distances made at Philadelphia, March, 1907.
† Previous best performance, 1905.

Hours.	Miles.*	Miles†	B. F. Edge, Green Napier.	H. C. Tryon and A. F. Browning, White Napier.	F. Draper and F. Newton, Red Napier.
1	44	41	71 mls 120 yds		
2	84	83	140 mls 1980 yds		
3	123	124	207 mls 800 yds		
4	155	160	271 mls 1160 yds		
5	199	198	342 mls 1350 yds		
6	231	238	407 mls 60 yds		
7	276	275	474 mls 360 yds		
8	307	306	537 mls 1210 yds		
9	349	344	609 mls 720 yds		
10	378	362	670 mls 1200 yds		
11	409	399	787 mls 480 yds		
12	440	429	799 mls 1600 yds		
13	469	460	866 mls 330 yds		
14	498	494	938 mls 480 yds		
15	529	523	1006 mls 1640 yds		
16	560	553	1068 mls 400 yds		
17	579	584	1139 mls 1100 yds		
18	609	616	1203 mls 800 yds		
19	641	651	1263 mls 1170 yds		
20	668	686	1327 mls 1190 yds		
21	703	724	1390 mls 1100 yds		
22	738	760	1458 mls 130 yds		
23	769	797	1579 mls 360 yds		
24	791	837	1581 mls 1310 yds	1538 mls 160 yds	1521 mls 80 yds

Mercedes arouses plenty of interest

two drivers. Their names deserve to go on record – Draper cum Newton and Tryon cum Browning. Edge's car travelled a little more than 1,581 miles in the twenty-four hours, an average speed of nearly 66mph. Although the cars were fitted with powerful acety-lene head-lamps they were little used, being ineffective on the vast expanse of concrete; instead, powerful flares studded the edges of the track. Taking everything into account, the strain on the unrelieved driver must have been formidable; the only moments of relaxation were during stops for fuel or tyres, when advantage was taken of a change of position by lying full-length flat on his back.

The triple performance was an amazing tribute to the quality of the Napier cars; throughout the runs no mechanical troubles were experienced. The same standard was not shared by the tyres, a total of sixty-one replace-ments being consumed by the three cars. Dividing the total equally between them, the average life per set will be seen as around seventy-five miles. There will also be seen the vast im-provements in tyres over the years, a result largely deriving from track-racing; yet, though improved out of all knowledge, tyres were long to remain a continuing if diminishing source of hazard to the racing driver. The more recent developments in racing, higher speeds over circuits demanding fan-tastic expertise in cornering, have proved even more searching. While bringing some benefit to the private motorist, it has tended to be an in-breeding process in aid of the pro-

fessional; the vital foundations were laid much earlier.

To one having experienced on road and track the uncertainties and dangers of the old beaded-edge type (bolstered up with security-bolts and a good supply of Seccotine glue on the beads) the progress in design and construction of tyres is among the wonders of the intervening years. As early as 1906 cars had attained a standard of mechanical reliability far exceeding the most optimistic to be expected of tyres. Witness of this was borne in the Michelin Guide of the same year in which was recommended, as essential to the enjoyment of any motor-tour, prior confirmation by telegrams from various points along the route to the effect that replacement tyres of the appropriate size would be available.

From the point of view of racing, there were two factors which mitigated to some extent the dangers attendant upon a blow-out; wheels were large in diameter and cross-sections of tyres were small. Instances were almost common when drivers would ignore a burst and continue to run on the rim of the wheel; only too often it did not work out; the outer cover would tear into strips, become wrapped round the axle and lock the

Nazzaro's Fiat 'Mephistopheles'

wheel solid. At anything over 70mph a blow-out could mean a fifty-fifty chance and every driver knew it.

In long-distance events, as on the occasion of the twenty-four hour run, an obvious precaution was to stop and change tyres before they were too badly worn. The Napier racing cars were among the first to exploit the time-saving device of detachable wheels – and wire-spoke wheels into the bargain. The use of wooden 'artillery' wheels was still quite common even for racing, but Brooklands soon disposed of that state of affairs. The introduction of these details was only the start; sustained high speed was to reveal an unending sequence of mechanical weakness previously unsuspected. In August 1908 Edge was challenged by the Italian driver Nazzaro and his monster Fiat, 'Mephistophelis' A 90hp Napier 'Samson' from the Edge stable and driven by Newton was to undertake the duel. Newton fought hard to beat Nazzaro at over 100mph only to be foiled by a broken crankshaft, owing to torsional vibration and metal fatigue.

So it was to go on, year after year. Maximum speeds would not go so very

much higher, perhaps another 20mph
or so; but by degrees speeds of over
100mph would be attained by progressively smaller and smaller engines.
Tyres would become less likely to
blow out and able to travel much greater
distances before being worn out.
Meanwhile, endless lessons would be
learned about petrol engines and
motor-cars in general; lessons which
would be absorbed and pondered over
by men who, in many cases, would rise
to positions of sufficient authority to
direct the trend of technical development on land, on sea and in the air.
Brooklands was not just a succession of
race-meetings; rather it was a melting-
pot and a hot-bed of technological
progress. Nevertheless, as already

**A competitor brakes hard after
crossing the Finishing–Line. In the
further distance can be seen the
Members' Banking 'lying in wait'
for the driver who fails to pull up in
time**

American White steam cars lining up for a race in 1907. The Test Hill is not yet completed

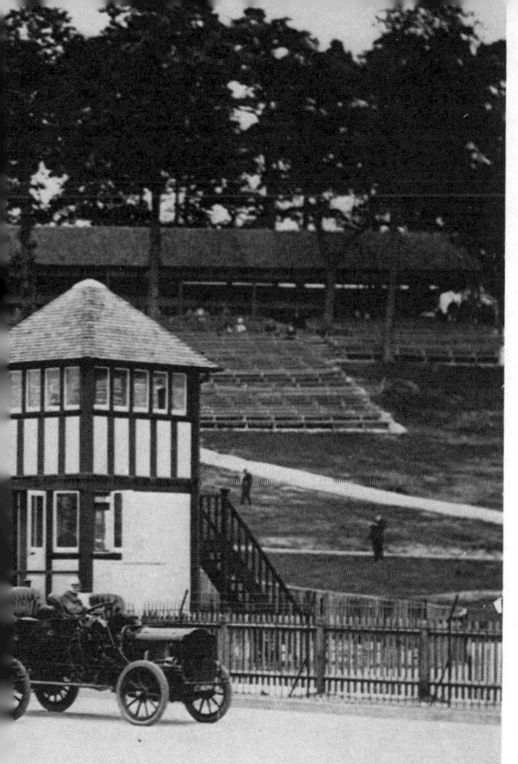

stated, the race-meetings were highly important.

The opening meeting was held on Saturday 6th July, 1907 when about 13,500 people came to watch. In view of the complete novelty of racing in this country and the wide publicity which had at last been given in the press during the later stages of construction, this gate was not considered particularly encouraging. There were other aspects which proved sources of disappointment. The public enclosures on the Members' Hill, graded in price according to situation and the opportunity of seeing the racing at close quarters, were too far from the inner edge to convey any adequate impression of speed. Not unreasonably, the best positions had been reserved for club members; to many of the others the cars looked like flies crawling along in the distance. It also happened

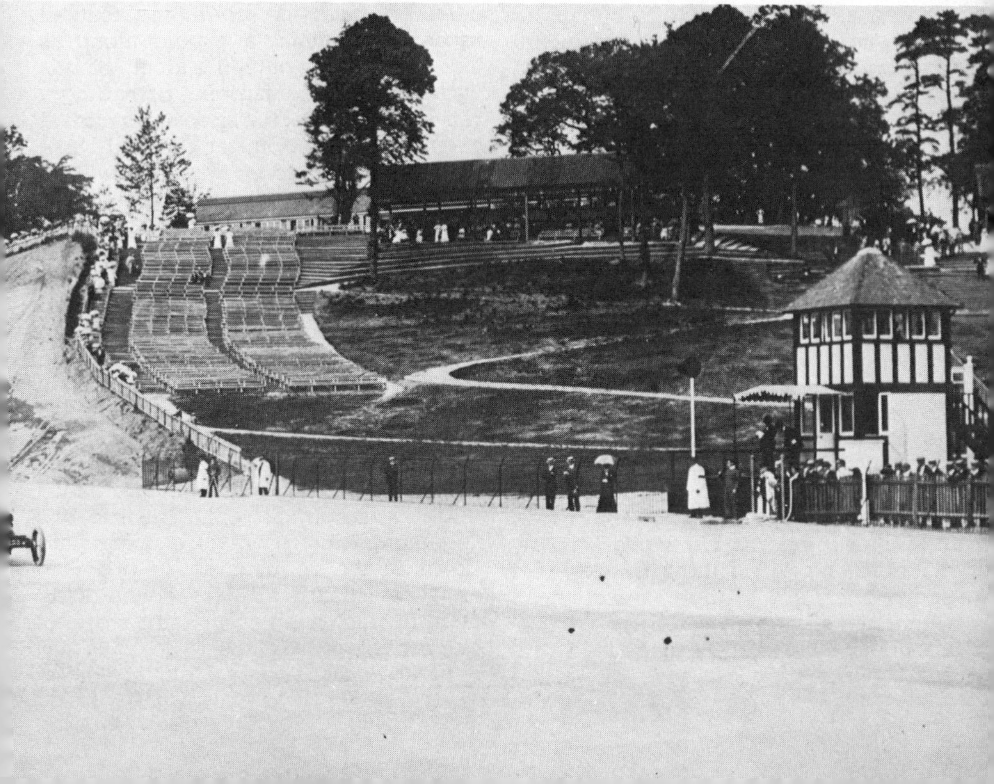

that the speeds this day were below those expected.

Much of this disappointment might have been mitigated if the general public had been permitted close-up views of the racing cars in the Paddock, but this area was strictly confined to competitors and their assistants. Worst of all, there prevailed a sense of being too loosely·controlled and marshalled, a condition ever repugnant to the British temperament; added to this, refreshment arrangements left much to be desired. The subsequent reper-cussions of all these deficiencies were to be magnified by unhappy relations between authority and representatives of the press. Some went so far as to describe this opening meeting as a 'flop'.

There is little reason to suppose that competitors had much cause for com-plaint. A good deal could be suffered against the prospect of substantial cash prizes; 1,400 golden sovereigns as first prize in a race of thirty laps was, to say the least of it, generous. It is not known whether this generous scale was merely a slavish copying of horse-racing practice or a calculated incen-tive considered necessary to entice the reluctant entrant. However, it was a scale which could not be maintained indefinitely if, in fact, it was ever necessary at all. Meanwhile, a fair proportion was to be won by members of the Napier 'twenty-four hour' team; at the opening meeting they were to win several firsts, a tie and a third. This does not mean that there was no effective opposition. Out of a field of twenty different makes they were parti-cularly hard pressed by two of them, Mercedes and Darracq; names which were to remain famous in motor-racing years after Napier cars had been with-drawn from racing.

All these early racing cars comprised little more than a bare chassis sur-mounted by a shallow bucket-seat (more often two of them) upholstered with a minimum of material; one driver is said to have entirely dispensed with this accessory and to have sat on the petrol-tank with only a piece of carpet in between. Steering-wheels would often occupy most unsuitable positions from the point of effective control and flooring reduced to a single board on which would rest the driver's heels. These were features obvious to the eye; more critical in terms of safety was the geometry of steering-linkage and suspension. Much of the design was completed by rule-of-thumb or calculated guess; component parts might have the requisite strength while being woefully deficient in rigidity. It will ever be a source of wonder that the early days of Brook-lands were so free from accident due to mechanical failure. The two fatalities which marked the first season's racing were the result of errors of judgement, responsibility for which must lie be-tween the authorities and the drivers concerned.

In order to understand what hap-pened it is necessary to return to the layout of the track. The name 'Finishing Straight' was given to the chordal section for the logical reason that it was intended from the beginning that all races should finish at a point along its length just short of the Paddock. Stands were erected at this point, providing a raised view point for spectators and, at ground level, a number of small work shops which could be rented. It will be remembered that this straight continued on to rejoin the main circuit by way of an abrupt left-hand turn.

It followed that a driver crossing the finishing line would see straight ahead of him and about 300 yards distant an expanse of the twenty-nine foot high banking. It was obviously important that, after crossing the line, a driver should decelerate rapidly enough to ensure an easy left-hand turn which would bring him close to the inner edge of the track; strict instructions regarding this procedure were laid down in the regulations. In order to assist retardation this last section of the straight was given an upward slope of one in twelve.

At a press interview, Colonel Holden

had expressed his complete confidence in these arrangements notwithstanding the general absence of front-wheel brakes in those days. Little margin was made to provide for either human error or mechanical failure, neither of which risks can ever be totally eliminated. There was not long to wait for this weakness to be revealed. The first car to be involved in an accident was a Darracq which got out of control through the driver's efforts to avoid collision with another car immediately after crossing the line. After a sequence of alarming gyrations, the car shot backwards up the banking and over the top. The driver stayed at the wheel and survived; his accompanying mechanic jumped out and was killed. In the other case, a Minerva was simply driven too fast while making the left-hand turn; with the result that the front wheels collapsed and caused the car to overturn on top of the driver who was killed. Fortune was further reversed by the mechanic being thrown clear.

During the next few years a number of other people were to mount the banking and disappear from sight at this point; among them was a racing motor-cyclist named Remington who suffered a jammed throttle on his 1,000cc Matchless. Fortunately, he sustained no serious injury. Eventually and rather belatedly, it came to be recognised that use of the straight for its original purpose was much too hazardous and likely to become still more so as speeds increased. The alternative adopted was to confine racing to the main circuit; this continued until, around the middle 1920s, the whole concept of Brooklands racing was to be enlarged.

Beginning with the 'formal' procession of cars which had brought the inaugural ceremonies to a close, an increasing number of people gained experience of driving round the new motorcourse and subsequently described their impressions. The uneven character of its surface, with its bumps and depressions, was a frequent source of comment rather than complaint; several people simply asserting the opinion that bumps far worse were to be found on the open road. Likewise in the matter of dust. Some complained of the prevalence of a 'vicious and biting dust which seared the skin and parched the throat;' again with the added observation that conditions could be far worse on the road. (This was probably a temporary phase in the teething stage of newly-laid concrete; during my first visit to the track in 1911 there was no evidence of any nuisance due to dust.)

Much more to the point were observations by the faster drivers regarding characteristics of the banking; on this subject there would appear to have existed considerable differences of opinion. Some expressed complete satisfaction whereas Mr Warwick Wright, after completing in his Darracq a lap timed by Moore-Brabazon at rather less than 90mph, suggested that speeds above 100mph would be impracticable and that 120mph would require another fifteen feet of banking. In fact, during the following year, Newton was to cover ten laps on his Napier at an average just above the hundred; a lap speed which in due course would become almost commonplace. In 1935, John Cobb would set the all-time high lap speed at 143mph!

The disparity between premature opinion and actual accomplishment serves to emphasise the vital degree to which Brooklands driving depended not only on experience but, above all, on the innate qualities of the individual. It was never a place where it could be said that 'what one man can do another can', as many of us were to find out. In this matter of using the banking to fullest advantage an exacting technique had to be acquired. It was one thing to locate the worst of the bumps and hollows; it was quite another to avoid or master them, especially when passing a somewhat slower car high up and close to the rim. Who, without fearless determination coupled with a measure of wizardry, could decide how near to the edge it would be safe to go – and

instantaneously act upon the decision ?
Yet even a proven master could make a
mistake as when in 1932 Clive Dunfee,
driving the new 8-litre Bentley and
about to pass a Bugatti, allowed one
wheel to pass over the edge and so
bring about tragic disaster.

With the benefit of hindsight and
some experience of engineering
design, one is left to wonder why there
was never incorporated in the original
design of the banking a near-vertical
curb a couple of feet high instead of
leaving the rim 'open'. Granted the
possibility of some disadvantage, it
might have saved Dunfee. Speculation
on such features is hampered by uncertainty regarding the detail cross-
section of the uppermost banking. An
article in a 1907 issue of *The Motor*
refers to the banking having a maximum slope of 1 in 1.6 ; assuming this to
be the tangent of the angle, this represents an inclination of thirty-two
degrees from the horizontal. A little
arithmetic will show that this angle
(assumed to occur on the Members'
Banking) would correspond to a speed
of about 97mph with no unbalanced
centrifugal force. A speed of 120mph
would require for the same condition a
slope of 1 to 1, or 45 degrees. Regarded
from this point of view the physical
effort, quite apart from the skill,
required to drive under the Members'
Bridge at 143mph may be left to the
imagination. But that is not all ; the
bumps must also be taken into account,
one of them perhaps the worst on the
whole course !

It is in such terms that the mastery
of the star drivers is to be measured.
When it is remembered that all who
drove were not in this category, it
might be supposed that the history of
Brooklands was a sequence of serious
accidents and fatalities. This is very far
from being the case ; it was much more
notable for its amazing escapes. Most
of the time a circuit was just one long
continuing ride in which the driver was

**Probably one of the world's first
petrol pumps**

saved from boredom by bone-shaking
discomfort. So long as nothing happened, it was easy to yield to the
intoxication of speed and push all
thoughts of unpleasantness into the
background. A sudden accident to a
friend could change all this in a moment
and it was in such circumstances that
the first great personality decided to
withdraw his team from racing.

Ever with an eye to maximum advertisement from every source, S F
Edge announced through a letter to
The Times, towards the end of 1908, his
intention of withdrawing the Napier
team from racing – on grounds that it
was becoming too dangerous. Many
were puzzled by the announcement
itself and the form of words in which it
was expressed. So far as I am aware, the
story behind this entirely unpremedi-
tated decision has never been told. It is
interesting from many points of view
and illuminates just one of that in-
finitude of strands which, taken altogether, make up that imponderable
phase of human experience which is
signified by the word 'Brooklands'. It
was told to me more than once by the
principal actor who, many years later
and during my long sojourn at Napier's,
became guide, philosopher and much-
loved friend.

As already recorded, among the
supporting drivers of the twenty-four
hour record attempt had been H C
Tryon. Soon after completing his
apprenticeship at a Lincolnshire firm of
agricultural engineers, he became
suddenly smitten by an irresistible
desire to enter the small but expanding
motor industry ; moreover, he had
made up his mind where he would
start. He wrote just one letter and that
was to Napier's ; it produced a blank
refusal. Determined not to take 'no'
for an answer, he travelled to the works
in London only to be refused admission
for interview by a surly commission-
aire. Pushing the man aside, he forced
his way into Montague Napier's private
sanctum. By sheer persistent pleading
he succeeded in being engaged on
trial at a very low salary. Within a few

60hp Itala and 40hp Iris machines of an early meeting

weeks he was testing cars and making constructive suggestions. Quite by chance, he attracted the attention of S F Edge who promptly secured his transfer to his own associated organisation; here he soon was put in charge of the racing team and virtually became Edge's technical adviser. After his successful début at Brooklands it was arranged that he should attempt some records on his own.

Despite a burst tyre, he was able to establish a new record for fifty miles at 80mph and then carried on to attempt the hour. Travelling high-up and towards the end of the Members' Banking, another tyre burst and the car lost control. After an alarming series of skids, spins and even

An early approach to streamlining on this 13.9 Chenard-Walcker

named Draper happened to be occupying the mechanic's seat; Draper suffered serious injuries which were to mark his face for life; the fact that these injuries implanted a permanent smile was little consolation.

The thought (quite unfounded) that he may have been responsible for his friend's predicament preyed on Tryon's mind to the extent that he could find no peace. In the end he came to what can only be described as an intense religious experience which, among other effects, left him convinced that racing must stop. But how was he to present the case to Edge? He was still pondering the question at the Burlington Street showrooms when Edge came into the office. 'Ah, Tryon! the very man I wanted to see,' he said, 'it is high time we were planning next year's racing programme. What are we going to do?' Without a moment's hesitation and (as he subsequently related) in words which did not seem to come of his own volition, Tryon replied 'We are not going to race any more; we will retire on our laurels!'

When the shock had subsided, both men felt that they had received a revelation although their points of view were far apart; Tryon had absolved his conscience, Edge had perceived a marvellous theme for future advertisements – 'By unbroken success in racing and all other competitions it has been proved that the Napier is the best car in the world' and there could be no point in proving it again. It was soon decided that Tryon would transfer back to the works where he was to serve for the next fifty years, making irreplaceable contributions to the evolution and development of a famous line of aero-engines. These contributions were to culminate in the apotheosis of the piston-type of internal combustion engine – the 'SABRE' which, installed in the Hawker 'Tempest' was to beat the menace of the flying-bomb. And it all began at Brooklands.

reversals, the car plunged to the inner edge, leapt off the track clean over the entrance road, finally coming to rest the right way up, though steeply inclined, on some rough ground below. Neither car nor driver was much damaged but Tryon was naturally very shaken. This and a number of equally disconcerting episodes were accepted as an occupational hazard. The crunch came when he crashed at a time when a team-mate

ROUND THE TRACK

The withdrawal of the Napier team was one of the highlights among various events which marked a period of change. With the team's departure there remained among the numerous and assorted field a number of individual cars and drivers receiving a measure of support from the manufacturers concerned, but the scale fell far short of the comprehensive teamwork which had been developed by S F Edge. Soon there would appear a better sustained if not more intense example of organised effort on the part of the Sunbeam and Vauxhall factories. There was also pending a marked expansion of the amateur element in consequence of the introduction of motor-cycle racing, also bringing in its trail a broadening of the social context of Brooklands. The May meeting of 1908 had been embellished by a handicap race exclusively confined to officers of H M Household Brigade of Guards; an event which might not have been so easily arranged had the entrants been required to compete on two wheels instead of four.

Sheer economics and the structure of society which distinguished the times had rendered inevitable a particular form of snobbery attaching to motor racing in the early days – exemplified by the posters proclaiming and inviting patronage from 'the right people'. The introduction of motor-cycle racing was to change all that and was to make Brooklands, for the rest of its life, an open society requiring no other passport but a passionate interest in speed.

A good deal of the credit for many improvements must be given to Colonel Lindsay Lloyd who in 1909 succeeded to the onerous duties of Clerk of the Course, responsible for the day-to-day control of the track. While never relaxing that minimum of discipline indispensable to the maintenance of good order, he could turn a blind eye to the things that did not really matter. The peculiarities of temperament which had marked his predecessor will be reserved for mention when dealing with the beginnings of British aviation. Under Lloyd's direction, many of those

irksome restrictions and inadequacies which had niggled the earlier crowds of spectators were abolished. Except on race days the use of the course was available to anybody willing to pay a shilling or two and desirous of trying their vehicles at speed; and even on race days the same facilities were open to spectators once the formal racing had finished. Among other reforms, the annual subscription to the BARC was reduced to two guineas.

In that same year of 1909 was formed the British Motor Cycle Racing Club (BMCRC), of which body I was proud to become a member in 1912. Membership of their body conferred exactly the same privileges – free use of all facilities throughout the year and inclusive of all race-meetings. There is little doubt that bringing the two forms of racing together was responsible for that atmosphere of genial freedom which was so characteristic a feature of life at Brooklands. Motor-cars found their original market through their obvious advantages over the 'carriage-and-pair' which had so long been the

Preparing to start—one of the earliest motor-cycle races at Brooklands in 1909

means of transport and a status symbol of both aristocracy and the leisured classes in general. It was inevitable that some of the trappings of social precedence should be reflected in the new sport of motor-racing. On the other hand, the origins of motor-cycle racing had been plebeian to a degree, tarnished by excessive intimacy with 'trade'. 'Trade' may be interpreted as the very antithesis of the aristocratic idea.

As earlier observed, the traditional custom whereby a gentleman indulged in horse-racing by the nomination of a professional jockey to do the actual riding was easily carried over into the field of motor-racing. No such tradition has ever existed whereby a gentleman owned a number of pedal-cycles and hired professional cyclists to ride them in competition. However, members of the cycle trade did exactly that. A brief résumé of these developments will

Clerk of the Course Colonel Lindsay Lloyd (driving)

illustrate the minor social revolution attaching to the history of the new course.

From the first days of the 'Ordinary' bicycle (popularly known as the 'Penny Farthing' on account of the gross inequality between front and rear wheel diameters), cycle-racing on the road was a highly respectable sport in which all classes of people could take part without any loss of status. The introduction of the 'Safety Cycle' (characterised by equality between diameters of the wheels) was followed by cut-throat competition between the various manufacturers. Each manufacturer sought the maximum advertisements of his products, but soon found that road-races through tracts of open countryside did not offer much opportunity. Accordingly, they turned to the small wood-boarded tracks where competitors circled in full view of large concentrations of people. Unfortunately, this form of cycle-racing soon became a hot-bed of doubtful practice and open to the sort of corruption and chicanery which the

horse-racing aristocracy, whatever their faults, would never have tolerated. It was in these inauspicious circumstances that motor-cycle racing made its début; not by way of direct competition but in the form of pacing machines in whose slip-stream a pedal-cyclist was able to attain fantastic speeds.

It did not take long to conceive the idea of races between the pace-makers; but these were big and clumsy machines deliberately designed to produce maximum disturbance (and therefore resistance) of the air. Soon there were brought to these boarded tracks machines closely resembling the standard types offered for sale to the public. From the beginning, this new form of racing remained entirely free from malpractice if only because, quite unlike the pedal-cycle industry, the individual makers were for the most part modest men in a small way of business. Moreover, instead of hiring other people they rode the machines themselves; nevertheless, to the general public any form of racing on two wheels tended to be suspect. It was therefore an act of some courage on the part of the authorities to bring motor-cycle racing to Brooklands.

Just as Napier cars had threatened to dominate the field of car-racing so, over much the same period, Matchless motor-cycles were predominant in their own sphere. These machines were manufactured by the firm of Collier & Sons, the senior member had been one of two partners in a prosperous (and then novel) steam-laundry for which he had designed and built the machinery. Impressed by the large profits attaching to the cycle industry, he proposed to his partner that the laundry business be diversified by adding the manufacture of cycles; the partner declined and remained to look after the laundry while Collier went off to make a fortune. It was the sons 'C R' and 'H A' who persuaded their father to go further and take up motor-cycles. It was also the two sons who swept the board at the first motor-cycle race meeting at Brooklands by winning at something over 70mph on their own make of machine. There was nothing surprising in this: they were used to winning races, from the boarded track at Canning Town to the Tourist Trophy Races in the Isle of Man.

I knew these men quite well and later spent a period of apprenticeship in their works. 'C R' was of slender build and bore some facial resemblance to Charlie Chaplin. 'H A' was a big man with heavy moustache and looked at the world through a substantially constructed pair of spectacles; these, in conjunction with the moustache, gave an impression of ferocity completely at variance with his kindly nature. Both were fearless riders and sound engineers into the bargain. They were also physically tough, as they had to be to survive the violent buffeting of machines completely devoid of any springing. 'Spring Forks' for front wheels were already on the market, but

Official timekeeper A V Ebblewhile (left) in his later years beside a Weymann-bodied Talbot

Above: 1913 Twin cylinder Dot JAP. Below: H A Collier on his twin-cylinder Matchless, 1910

Above: Horizontally-opposed twin-cylinder Douglas, 1920. Below: J Emerson on his horizontally-opposed ABC twin, 1920

Differing ideas in the construction of early streamlined bodies

these still young veterans of the board track (where they were not really necessary) would as yet have none of them, believing that they would result in too great a loss of transverse rigidity. Once again, Brooklands was to teach its lessons; sprung front-forks were very soon universal.

During its first few years the BARC included one or two motor-cycle events in their programmes, with a view to adding interest and breaking the monotony. BMCRC meetings were held monthly during the season, these being exclusively confined to two wheels and occasionally three. This specialisation allowed wide variety in the duration of races, from a single lap to as much as 200 miles. The number of starters in a race might be as few as five or as many as fifty; with the larger fields a simultaneous standing start provided an awe-inspiring spectacle to spectators and riders alike. Before 1914, clutches and gear-boxes were

nearly unknown on motor-cycles, the rear wheel being driven directly by the engine through the medium of a rubber and canvas belt.

It was this mechanical austerity which compelled the rider to push and run alongside the machine, with the exhaust-valve lifted from its seating in order to reduce resistance from cylinder compression. When sufficient speed had been attained, the exhaust control-lever would be released and, with luck, the engine would burst into life; at this point, and not a moment later, (otherwise the handle-bars might be wrenched from his grasp) the rider would leap into the air and vault into the saddle. Failure of the engine to fire could reduce the rider to a stage of physical exhaustion. High compression-ratio, big valve-overlaps and large-bore chokes all combined to make starting more difficult and uncertain; yet all three were required for maximum speed.

The present purpose being to present to the reader a broad picture of the nature and deeper purposes of life at Brooklands rather than to attempt a detailed step-by-step account of an endless series of races, all of them alike in general pattern, it would seem advantageous from time to time to turn to the frankly autobiographical. Whether a young novice or an experienced master, whether on two wheels or four (or even three), the sensations of racing round the circuit were basically the same. Besides, I was far from being alone in yielding to the irrestistible lure of the track at so tender an age and in allowing nothing to hinder a closer acquaintance at the earliest possible moment. Time and again, with variations, their story would be mine.

My first visit was in the capacity of spectator at the age of fifteen in the hot summer of 1911. For some considerable time previously, academic study had competed with intense absorption in the pages of *Motor Cycling, The Autocar* and every other periodical of similar interest which might come to hand. The unexpected present of a half sovereign inspired allowed me to see in the flesh those men and machines whose appearance and achievements were already familiar to me through the printed page. From the moment of arrival at Weybridge station, everything came fully up to expectation without a vestige of disillusionment. Walking across the heath there could clearly be heard at intervals the bark and roar of engine exhaust. Once through the turnstiles, the whole place was open to be roamed at will except for the actual circuit. It was a BMCRC meeting with all races starting and ending at the Fork. After a spell at this point, closely studying the various techniques displayed in starting and then watching the machines as they went by on succeeding laps, I made a general tour of inspection. A view from the top of the Test Hill revealed the immensity of the establishment, then down to the Paddock to look inside one or two of the rentable workshops. So avid had been my earlier reading that it almost felt as though I had seen it all before. Tired out, I went up to the balcony of the club house and had an excellent tea for a shilling; by way of added value was the opportunity of a chance word with one or two of the regular habitués sitting at the table. Whether I had been entitled to enter these inner precincts at all was something I never knew; nobody seemed to bother. The dominating impression everywhere was one of free and easy friendliness.

The following spring I was able to return as a competitor. Positioned near the middle of some thirty or forty competitors spaced across the whole hundred foot width of the track at the Fork, I tensely awaited the signal to start. Away to the left and in front stood a notable figure, A V Ebblewhite who for many years to come would continue to function as chief-starter and time-keeper; his left-arm was extended horizontally and in his hand a small flag; the dropping of this flag would be the signal to go. Although I had never been round the circuit before, the possibility of any surprises being in store never occurred to me, so intensely had the situation been imagined. The correct technique was believed to be simple enough – to get away smartly and make a bee-line for the inner edge of the track; the closer one got, the shorter the distance to be covered, all official distances being measured on a line fifty feet from the inner edge. The present race was for a hundred miles, the equivalent of thirty-seven laps.

At last the flag dropped and immediately the scene was transformed. Three dozen young men were heaving their heavy machines forward and running as fast as they could go. In a very few seconds there was bedlam; first a few, one after another, and then the whole mass of engines burst into life. As the riders leapt into their saddles, motor-cycles swerved dangerously close to one another and for a few moments a number of collisions seemed inevitable. As my own engine sprang into life the competitor on the

In the heatwave of 1914 some competitors relax in the River Wey

right swerved in front, missing my wheel by inches as he made towards the inside. For my own part, once safely in the saddle all thought of the inside line vanished into thin air; it was one thing to know the correct proceedure, it was another to carry it out. Quite apart from the fact that everybody displayed the same intention, my machine bucketed about in the most unexpected manner and every effort was required to keep it on a straight course. In my untutored innocence I had imagined that the surface of the course would be quite smooth.

The difficulties were accentuated by the need to juggle with the pair of levers which controlled the carburettor. It was not simply a matter of opening the throttle. Motor-cycle carburettors possessed both a throttle lever and another lever which controlled the strength of the petrol/air mixture. Then there was the ignition advance-and-retard lever, this one situated on the side of the petrol tank about which my knees were tightly gripped; otherwise it would have been impossible to remove one hand from the handle-bars. As we climbed the one in thirty incline towards the curve round the Members' Hill, most were doing about 50mph but varying our speeds sufficiently to space ourselves out: the inside edge was now becoming more accessible.

Still much disconcerted to find the going so rough, I settled down to take things as they came. There was not long to wait. Sweeping round the long bend and under the Members' Bridge, all the time the way overshadowed by the high Members' Banking on the right and the hill on the left, I became aware of going downhill as the speed rose perceptibly.

Emerging from this hundred foot wide ravine, there came into view the whole vast expanse of Brooklands, the Railway Straight commencing in the immediate foreground and stretching far ahead. It was an inspiring sight and a memorable moment; it was only a second later when it became yet more memorable but distinctly less inspiring. There came a sudden thrust from the left and in response the machine veered to the right, accompanied by a wobbling of the front wheel and handle-bars. I was in a cold sweat, heightened by the attainment of maximum speed (about 65mph) as the bottom of the one in twenty-five incline was passed. Beginning the long straight beside the railway embankment the machine became stable and the bumps less troublesome.

The temporary deviation had been caused by sudden exposure to a south-west wind on emerging from the shelter of the Members' Hill. The strength of the wind that day was relatively light, its effect much exaggerated by my own stupidity. It was a requirement of regulations that motor-cycles should carry on each side a circular disc of twelve inches diameter, painted black and bearing the competitor's number in bold white figures. A man with a brush and a bucket of whitewash was posted in the Paddock for this particular duty. In my inexperience, I had bolted my number-plates to the front-forks with the result that even a moderate wind-pressure had produced a marked turning-moment on the front wheel assembly. This explanation not being immediately apparent, the incident was a source of worry. It may be added that when a really strong south-west wind was blowing the sudden impact could be a considerable hazard no matter where the number-plates might be situated; to the unwary even a racing-car was not immune. As a matter of fact Louis Coatalen, the famous designer and driver of Sunbeam cars, had given a vivid description and warning of this danger in the pages of *The Autocar* but I had missed it.

The journey down the railway straight was not marked by any similarly untoward event; which was just as well because there was plenty to contend with. The motor-cycles of those days depended upon the timely operation of a hand-pump for their lubrication; failure in its proper operation could result in engine seizure, causing in turn a serious skid or even the propulsion of the rider over the handle-bars. At touring speeds one pumpful every ten miles would normally be sufficient; at racing speeds, very much more because so much oil was thrown out of the exhaust pipe. Without experience, which might be bought dearly, it was difficult to decide how many pumpfuls should be given during each lap; too little would mean seizure, too much would oil up the sparking-plug. It was a difficult decision to take for quite a different reason; operation of the pump meant taking one hand off the handle-bars. It was not too bad when the pump was fitted with a non-return valve and the plunger returned under the action of a spring; one hand was required for only a few seconds in one single operation. The more common case of a simple pump, worked in conjunction with a hand-operated two-way cock and requiring four consecutive operations extending over twenty seconds, could be a veritable nightmare. Hitting a bad bump with one hand off the handle-bars was a combination of events to be avoided.

After the Railway Straight came the long, almost semi-circular curve of the Byfleet Banking; it seemed almost interminable. Soon the aeroplane sheds and hangars were visible just beyond the inside edge; I had never seen them before and this was hardly the occasion to begin. Then came the narrow bridge over the track which gave access to the flying-ground; after that had been passed the circuit was monotonous apart from the discomfort. At last, the banking came to an end and the Fork could be seen ahead; its passing would register the end of the first lap. As all the asides will have tended to distortion of the time-scale, it should be mentioned that this lap had taken just less than three minutes.

To a spectator, the sections both before and after the Fork might well appear to lie in a straight line; in fact, they formed a slightly re-entrant curve. This curvature was just noticeable on a motor-cycle doing 60mph; to a car doing twice that speed it could be a source of anxiety in aiming for the best point of approach to the Members' Banking. The problem was accentuated by the presence of one of the worst bumps in the whole course, the other being at the end of the Members' Banking where the track was incorporated in a bridge spanning the River Wey; it was worse the higher one went up the banking. Speeding past the Fork, there could be seen on the left the crowd of spectators; close by, the judges' box. Later on, officials would be accommodated rather more comfortably on the other side of the track close to where the Vicker's Sheds would also appear.

Above: The famous (and infamous) 'bump' at the end of the Members' Banking. Below: An excellent point of vantage from which the racing could be seen. In the foreground is the '10 feet' line on which motor–cycle records were measured. Right: The Members' Bridge spanning the Members' Banking.

Above: Model T Fords beneath the Members' Bridge. Below: August 1908 – Lane's Mercedes hit the parapet at an estimated 100mph before an audience of 7000

Within the first lap, the compact mass of the other competitors had diffused into an attenuated line. Being in line and usually close to the inner edge, one saw little ahead beyond the man immediately in front except on the Byfleet Banking where it was possible to see across to a few riders curving off to the left. During the first lap I was overtaken by one or two whose getaway had been even slower than my own; it was only after a few more laps that the really fast machines came by after completing one more lap than myself. The race included several classes of engine ranging from 250cc to 1,000cc twins. Alas, there was soon coming a time when there would be ample opportunity of watching the other competitors.

At about the ninth or tenth lap, apart from feeling tired, I had really settled down; but without warning there came a stunning blow on my back, my machine went into a skid and stopped almost abruptly. The driving-belt had broken and become wedged between the belt-rim and a rear tubular member of the frame; it was this jamming which had caused the skid and allowed the free end of the belt to hit me in the back. It was towards the end of the Railway Straight that it happened and, fortunately, near the inner edge; otherwise I might have been hit by something more substantial. Not only had the belt broken, but one half of the fastener had become stuck in the groove of the engine pulley; in consequence, the spare belt entwined about my middle after the fashion of an army officer's Sam Browne belt was useless. There was nothing to be done except to walk, pushing the machine all the way to the Fork, a distance of about a mile and a half, most of it along that interminable Byfleet Banking First of all, the back wheel had to be freed and this took quite a time.

For a day in March it was unusually warm and, from time to time, it was desirable to stop and rest; this afforded ample opportunity to observe the more fortunate competitors in action. Far and away the fastest was one Arthur Moorhouse riding a 1,000cc Indian twin; with unfailing regularity he would pass about halfway up the banking although his speed was not more than about 75mph. In the course of this race he was to break the existing one-hour record. At the next meeting, the following month, he met his death along the Railway Straight by hitting a telegraph post in which remained the imprint made by the impact of his goggles. The cause was never established although it may be surmised. Despite the fact that Indians were fitted with automatic mechanical lubrication of the engine, an automatic (single control) carburettor, its throttle operated (as in the case of ignition advance/retard) by twist-grips instead of awkward levers, Moorhouse was in the habit of riding with only one hand on the handle-bars while he fiddled with something or other on his engine.

Equally prominent, although for a different reason, was a Captain Miller who after the First World War became manager of the Wolseley racing-car stable; he was riding a 1,000cc Matchless which was apparently proving a little intractable. One moment he would fly past, very high on the banking and travelling at a good 80mph. Then, quite suddenly he would swoop down and come to a standstill. During my long trek round the Byfleet Banking, he reappeared several times doing the same thing. On the final occasion he spoke to me, giving me a characterisitcally frank opinion of his mount. My personal view is that either some part of the structure had worked loose or was grossly out-of-line.

By the time the Fork had been reached, I was in company with a number of other unfortunates pushing their machines. The pushers were an assorted lot, two professionals and the rest amateurs, one little older than myself, all of them inspired by the indomitable spirit of Brooklands, the determination to try again and do better next time.

GIANTS OR PIONEERS

An indomitable determination to try again and do better next time was indicative of an admirable attitude of mind and one indispensable for success; by itself, however, it was unlikely to achieve very much. Success at Brooklands depended upon two factors entirely distinct – familiarity with the circuit and the performance of one's mount. Closely bound up with these diverse factors were differences between amateur and professional. Familiarity with the course was equally accessible to both, it was only a matter of spending sufficient time; performance of one's mount was quite a different matter. The amateur was limited by what he could buy and the skill which he could devote subsequently to the tuning of the engine; the difference of initial outlay between car and motor-cycle would be substantial, but the practicable expenditure on tuning was likely to be much the same for both, the major difference being time: six or four components to be worked on as against only two or one. So far as motor-cycle racing was concerned, the amateur was for long to hold his own against the professional for the simple reason that both would be riding substantially the same types of machine; standard types which would differ in performance solely by the quality of skill in tuning which had been brought to bear.

If car racing had followed the same lines and remained primarily an amateur affair, improvement of the breed would have been greatly retarded. Apart from the great juggernauts of twenty or thirty litres capacity, the limit in miles per hour was never something to be bought over the counter or in the dealer's showroom; it demands a complex organisation of engineers and craftsmen, all working under one directing mind. If we examine the lists of entries in the first two years of Brooklands, we find cars with engines so big that the driver was bound to be capable of travelling very fast. Thus, it was possible for a 'gentleman of means' to purchase such a car and either drive it himself or arrange for someone to drive it on his behalf. It was essentially a sporting enterprise, comparable with

horse racing; gentlemen did not seek advertisement.

It would have been very remarkable if S F Edge had remained the only exception to the rule. After all, motor racing did not begin with the opening of Brooklands in 1907; it had been going on over the roads of Europe since the Paris-Bordeaux race of 1895. That race was inspired not so much by trade rivalry as by the desire of the pioneer makers to demonstrate to the world the possibilities of motor-cars in general. The earliest phase of competition derived from rivalry between nations, particularly France and Germany. There was also prominent, at least for a time, the element of stardom where individual drivers basked in public adoration with little regard to make or country of origin of the cars which they drove with such masterly skill and contempt for danger. As the dangers became increasingly manifest and speeds progressively increased, organisers of races sought to reduce average speeds by imposing various restrictions affecting the design of the cars; among the means chosen were

Starting line on the Railway Straight

weight of vehicle, fuel consumption and cubic capacity of engine.

It is to be noted that entries to the first BARC meeting were classified according to the bore of engine cylinders (in effect setting a limit to capacity), each class having to conform to a limitation of minimum weight. There were already in existence cars coming within these various categories. From a strictly sporting point of view, it was only fair that the smaller cars should not have to compete against the monsters. The arrangement also offered extended fields of advertisement – what great prestige and publicity could be gained by a car of low cylinder capacity outshining the performance of those in a higher category? From these various roots was to develop a continuing struggle towards more and more power from every litre of engine capacity until, so far as Brooklands was concerned, a nadir would be reached when a diminutive Austin Seven would be lapping the track at speeds little

Above: Another exercise in early streamlining – one of Alastair Miller's successful racing Wolseleys. Below: One of Coatalen's 1921 Grand-Prix Sunbeams. Segrave on the left

Above: A J Hancock in the Vauxhall on the record attempt, 30th August 1913.
Below: A J Hancock at the wheel of the 21hp Vauxhall. This starting-line was
situated on the Railway Straight and much used for record-breaking

short of those achieved by the early giants.

Such vast strides would entail years of effort on the part of design offices, workshops and experimental departments supported by an expanding development of scientific research. Each stage of progress would take time and quite a lot of money. Each individual type of car at any particular stage would need months of design, manufacture and testing before its first appearance on the starting line. Many companies would enter upon this gruelling work, only a few would persist to the end and achieve unqualified success. Some of these few would stay in racing for a time and then abandon the game in order to concentrate all their resources on mass-production of products bearing little superficial resemblance to the cars which had established the firms' reputations, yet nevertheless embodying the lessons which had been so expensively purchased. Then would come the last phase, the Bentleys; standard cars constitutionally capable of the highest speeds and, with them, the 'Bentley Boys' blessed with enough money to race them.

At various times throughout the whole period, there would be seen a number of individual and very specialised types fitted with huge aero-engines; late revivals of the monster idea though greatly refined in many respects. The financial and industrial arrangements which enabled these hybrids to be built and raced would be difficult to describe and in any case were the private concern of those involved. Right through the history of motor racing, the distinction between amateur and professional has been difficult to define. In the light of history, the matter is of no importance; amateur and professional alike have made great contributions to the development of the motor car.

During the first two years of Brooklands, a total approaching a hundred different makes of car were entered at various times; nearly half of them were of British origin. Many of their names would soon disappear from the programme except for an occasional entry by some private owner; about half a dozen would remain consistently regular competitors. Three names, at times separately and at times in conjunction, would figure over the whole period from the opening until the closing of the track – Sunbeam, Talbot and Darracq. For present purposes, the name Sunbeam is deserving of special attention because through the sequence of various models may be gained some insight into the development of the racing car at Brooklands, especially during the early and middle periods. The history of the Sunbeam is indissolubly linked with the name of Louis Coatalen, for so long its chief designer and on many occasions its exponent of the track. Yet Coatalen might never have gone half as far without the constant stimulus and provocation of another famous combination – Vauxhall and its chief designer L H Pomeroy (not to be confused with his late-lamented and gifted son).

In common with all the others, the first Sunbeams and Vauxhalls to race were standard models having their engines highly tuned to give improved performance. These engines, being based largely on rule-of-thumb evolved from pioneer days, set severe limits to the improvement obtainable. As time progressed, much was being learned about the internal-combustion engine from hard experience; still more from theoretical study of the subject on the part of a few highly able engineers whose range of thought was not inhibited by the day-to-day distractions of direct involvement in manufacture. Notable among these engineers was a certain Dr Lanchester.

As has so often happened in the course of engineering history (not least noticeably in the field of aviation), the publication of Lanchester's far-sighted conclusions was frequently ignored by the very people who could most have benefited from their study, namely contemporary designers.

Among the more enlightened were Coatalen and Pomeroy who realised that by suitable design much greater power could be obtained from a given size of engine. They were further stimulated by observing a vital trend in the development of the newly-invented aeroplane – the continuing reduction of air-resistance. Vauxhall racing cars were among the first (if not, in fact, *the* first) to achieve a considerable increase of speed simply by the provision of a body whose shape resulted in substantial reduction of air-resistance. Coatalen was not slow in following the lead.

Fundamentally, the maximum speed of a racing car (or any other vehicle for that matter) is determined by the ratio between engine power-output and the resistance to motion of the vehicle through the air; in consequence, reduction of air-resistance is equivalent to increase of engine power. It is possible to fit a new body in a very much shorter time than is required to design, make, test and perfect a new engine. Both designers having taken the first course proceeded with the second. With the aid of a new body alone, the Vauxhall car was enabled to be the first of its class to exceed 100mph. It is quite astonishing to reflect upon the omission on the part of those who designed the early monster cars to provide them with at least some pretension towards a streamlined body. The basic principles involved had been known for years past whereas, looking at the old photographs, it is difficult to imagine an outline more wasteful of power than that which typified the early giants. Not only was no attempt made to streamline the car, but the whole structure was high up from the ground and the driver's body largely exposed at an even higher level, thus increasing resistance still further.

The designs for the new engines were not conceived with the primary objective of Brooklands in mind; both firms were heavily committed to road racing on the Continent. Whereas a whole range of alternative classes for different sizes of engines would have permitted of choice in the former case, entries to the road races were restricted to engine capacities below some specified maximum. It was in this way that the endless struggle for more and more power from every litre of cylinder capacity began. Over the last sixty years, the rate of progress in this direction has been phenomenal. If the course of this accelerating progress is to be appreciated, let alone understood, it will be necessary to enter into some technical detail.

Stated in the simplest terms, the problem of obtaining maximum power from a given cylinder capacity can be reduced to achieving three objectives: the highest possible speed of rotation, the highest possible average gas-pressure and the reduction of all friction to a minimum. The limiting values of these three factors will be determined by the designer. Out of purely commercial and economic considerations, the quantity and quality of work carried out in the course of manufacture of standard production models will fall short of the extremely high standards which would be necessary to attain the limiting values of the design. In the interests of economy, surfaces will be left unmachined; fits and tolerances will be based on convenience rather than perfection, and so forth. It was this gap between the ideal and the commercially practicable, much greater in the early days than now, which offered both amateur and professional so much hope in the activity then known as tuning.

Perseverance and facility in the use of hand-tools could effect quite startling improvement in the performance of standard models, most of it through the elimination of avoidable friction. There was more than one habitué of Brooklands reliably credited with being able to dismantle any engine and, without replacing any component parts, rebuild it and thereby increase its power-output by anything up to ten per cent. Further increases were obtained by

Above : The early days of Brooklands could be relaxing for the spectator
Below : Women were much in evidence even before the Great War

filing and polishing all the internal walls of the inlet and exhaust passages, thus permitting of better filling and scavenging of the cylinders and so increasing the average gas-pressure. Given access to a lathe, cylinder-flanges could be skimmed in order to raise the compression-ratio, again to the same end. Lone amateur or organised works-team, all engaged in these arduous and exacting processes; there was no alternative except a new design.

Of course, there was much more involved than that. Carburation was for long looked upon as a kind of black art and many carburettors left much to be desired, their correct adjustment requiring considerable experience. Ignition systems had still a long way to go towards their ultimate development and to many were something of a mystery. It was a situation productive of the self-styled 'expert' and even the charlatan who professed to know how to win races but never racing himself. There was a good deal of talk about 'secrets of tune' and Temple Press even published a small book which bore that very title; it was an excellent publication serving chiefly to show that

there were no secrets after all; it was just full of common sense. Much light was to be thrown on these matters as a byproduct of the long-sustained rivalry between the Sunbeam and Vauxhall concerns. Their respective chief designers did not confine their competition to the race track, but at intervals sustained a continuing debate in the columns of the motoring-press regarding the pros and cons of alternative design features and trends.

Before passing to more detailed consideration of the racing cars produced by these designers, it would seem important to emphasise one aspect which distinguished the evolution of the modern motor-car, namely, that that evolution is not to be traced through any sequence of clever and original inventions. With the possible exception of the automatic transmission, nearly all the principles of the modern car were known in principle at the turn of the century; many progressive ideas, perfectly sound in their basic conception, were tried and often discarded in the early days only to be reintroduced with great success many years later. When these men set about designing new engines, with the intention of obtaining more power per litre of cylinder capacity than had ever been achieved before, they were not inventing but making what seemed to them an optimum choice from a number of known combinations of component parts.

This is in no way intended to belittle their competence or power of resource; it is just one of the facts of life. As has been remarked elsewhere, if components such as valves, pistons and suchlike were taken from two engines designed respectively in 1910 and 1970, and the opposite numbers photographed by a camera slightly out of focus, it might be very difficult to distinguish one photograph from the other. Yet there would be a vast difference between their performance and durability. Moreover, the history of transformation from one to the other could never be made visual; it might well be traced through the history of Brooklands.

Louis Coatalen was a popular figure at Brooklands, where he spent a great deal of time between the race meetings in which he was a regular competitor. He was always ready to talk (and to listen) to anyone deeply interested in engines, cars and racing; he was free in the expression of his own ideas and by no means averse to making use of other people's. By the middle of 1914, he had raced a variety of different Sunbeams, nearly all of the side-valve variety; he also established a number of records. These side-valve engines were basically standard types which had been highly tuned; with one of 16hp rating he approached 75mph whereas the same type untuned and as sold to the public was about 20mph slower. Personal participation in races was really something of a sideline; much more important from his point of view were the facilities which Brooklands offered for day-to-day testing of those specially-designed cars which

achieved considerable success in Continental races. In 1912, two French races – the Grand Prix and, within it, the Coupe de L'Auto – ended with Sunbeams first, second and third in the latter and fourth and fifth in the former: quite an outstanding performance.

Unlike the case of track racing, road races were by no means always won by the car capable of the highest speed; all sorts of other factors are – and always were – involved, many of them dependent upon body design just as much as upon the engine. Coatalen was a brilliant all-round designer; most of all he enjoyed designing engines and produced a good number in his time. He was far-seeing enough to design engines with a view to meeting the prospective demand for higher-powered aeroplanes. In this exacting field he was to encounter difficulties arising from his own brilliance. Meanwhile, he was to install his first 12-cylinder prototype in a new chassis which, in the hands of Chassagne (sometimes with others in support), was to break many records.

In close competition with the side-valve Sunbeams were several Vauxhall cars driven at Brooklands by some of the maker's senior executives; Kidner, the managing director being one of them. Kidner, in addition to other virtues, was a great sportsman and held in considerable regard by his employees; his retirement following upon the take-over by General Motors was the subject of much regret. At the time, I was a member of a small design team working on a special project and he would occasionally look in to discover the state of progress. It was easy to draw him into reminiscences of earlier days, whose passing he would have hindered had he been able. I suppose he had to go; he was out of sympathy with the times and reluctant to accept the more utilitarian outlook of his successors. Although his staff had played a leading part in introducing the synchromesh gear change to British cars, he confessed to us how much he deplored the passing of the 'crash' gear change with which, he argued, went half the pleasure of driving a car!

It was A J Hancock, works manager during the years which initiated the company's vast expansion, who was the most successful exponent of Vauxhall cars at Brooklands and elsewhere. He made his first track win in 1908; a year later, he introduced the first streamlined body and with its aid increased the speed of his car from not much more than 60mph to 80mph. Not long afterwards, with an improved model he just topped the 'hundred'.

All this time, of course, many other drivers in a great variety of cars were winning or losing races, breaking records or just circling an otherwise unoccupied track in pursuit of their own private or trade purposes. On many a week day the track might be entirely empty for hours at a time except for the odd workman or member of the staff who had some job to do. There would usually be a few people at work in the rented sheds or garages, taking engines to pieces and putting them together again, ever in search of a little more speed. Then, perhaps, a car would be heard coming from the entrance road into the Paddock. Stopping for a moment to look around, the driver would pass on through the gate giving on to the Finishing Straight; then the exhaust note would break into a succession of crescendoes as the driver accelerated after every gear change, the noise growing progressively less penetrating. A minute or so later the car would be seen (and heard) coming off the end of the Members' Banking onto the Railway Straight. Two or three laps, or maybe half a dozen, and he would be back in the Paddock only to disappear the way he had come; he alone knowing what it was all about.

Another might park for a time in the Paddock and retire into the club house for a meal in the restaurant or a discussion with the Clerk of the Course. Just as likely, he might leave his car only to wander round in the hope of finding someone with time to spare to discuss racing or the present state of the track. Quite different would be the arrival of some famous car or well-known driver; through the underground telegraph the Clerk of the Course would have been advised of the approaching visitor and would be down in the Paddock to greet him. It was usually the motor-cycles which arrived by way of descending the Test Hill, bypassing the Paddock on their way to the circuit. What really attracted attention from people who seemed to spring from nowhere was the sound and sight of someone going up the Test Hill. For some reason or other it was regarded as just a little eccentric.

Whatever might be happening, or even if nothing were happening at all, the predominating atmosphere of Brooklands was a sense of complete freedom to do what one liked. Yet no one entered Brooklands unobserved. Anyone arriving in an old banger would never get past the Paddock gates without receiving express permission from authority. One was free to do what one liked, but with two provisos – a reasonable degree of order must be maintained and nothing allowed which might impair safety on the course. There was great diversity of interesting people who came and went at Brooklands whether they appeared on Lists of Entrants or not; in the limited space available they must pass unrecorded. In any case, the present purpose is not to present a chronological history but to attempt an overall picture of what went on and the purposes which were served.

What could be seen to be going on was, like the iceberg, a fraction compared with the underlying mass. A driver such as we have just imagined, coming out of the blue and disappearing as soon as he had completed a few laps, might easily have been making an initial snap speed-test of a new type on which designers, works staff and others had been working intensively over a period of months. In fact, his deliberate shunning of conversation would lend much support to the idea; competition between the then much larger number of independent manufacturers was so keen, and their experimental projects shrouded with so much secrecy that, in addition to measures which would disguise a new model, a false beard might be provided for the driver. Manufacturers spent large sums of money on racing and record breaking so that they might advertise their successes; the last thing they wished to advertise was failure.

If Hancock was the principal exponent of Vauxhalls, the power behind him was Pomeroy. I never met him; he had left the firm some years before my period at Luton. The omission was not as important as might be supposed, for his influence could still be felt long after he had gone. If the parallel be admissable, it may fairly be said that in kind, if not in degree, Pomeroy remained for a number of years to Vauxhall what Nelson has remained for nearly two centuries to the British navy. At the very least, he established an enduring tradition and very few chief-engineers or chief-designers have succeeded in doing that. It is extremely doubtful if the same could be said of Louis Coatalen.

Brooklands was not the only field where these two great designers competed the one against the other; there were also France and the Isle of Man, not to mention another kind of competition through the pages of the motoring press. Here they would argue about bores and strokes and piston speeds and many another technical subject. As an aspiring designer, I learned many things which never could be learned through textbooks. Much of the force behind this correspondence derived from their preparatory work on completely new designs which would ultimately appear in the Isle of Man Tourist Trophy race and, a month later, in the French Grand Prix.

The design of motor-cars has ever tended to follow some prevailing fashion; whether it has been synchromesh or some other variation in transmissions, the sequence of battery – magneto – battery, shoe-brakes or hydraulically-operated discs, or even trends in body shape, the process has been the same. First one or two pioneers appear, their efforts ignored for years; then, in a period of months, universal adoption of their ideas by industry. It was much the same with racing cars. Multiple valves, overhead camshafts (single or twin), twin sparking plugs and dual ignition systems; all these and many other features had been introduced by original minds in the early days of racing. Being new ideas, they rarely contributed to victory. Where fashions are concerned it is not enough for an idea simply to exist; it has got to be demonstrated and 'sold': a process described as 'setting a trend'. At the time now under review, the great trend-setter in the sphere of racing cars was the French firm of Peugeot; their outstanding successes during 1913 set the seal of approval on a number of ideas tried long ago and subsequently discarded.

It is said that Coatalen bought the winning Peugeots and copied the engines in detail. However that may be, Pomeroy took the opposite course; he made a careful assessment of what had been done and applied his own experience towards what he believed would be an even better design. In actual fact it was, but several years would pass before it was proved. In the races for which they had been designed his cars were a great disappointment; due to grossly inadequate preparation, the cars were not completed until a few days before the first race. On the other hand, a Sunbeam came in first in the Tourist Trophy and third in the Grand Prix. It is important to note that the winner in this second race was a Mercedes, not only by virtue of being the fastest car in the field but still more through painstaking preparation and superb organisation.

In the above paragraph lies sufficient substance for several instructive sermons on the nature of engineering

View of the Test Hill – the car is a de-Dietrich

design and the art of motor racing, but most rewarding would be a series preached on those various aspects vitally affected by time. The absolute necessity of adequate time for preparation needs little explanation, applying as it does to nearly every activity; in this direction it is easily possible to estimate how much time will be required. There is another direction where it is quite impossible. However good a design may be it is never possible to foresee just how long it is going to take to turn it into a reliable mechanism. This is a truth which racing at Brooklands was just as likely to conceal as it was to reveal. The essential requirement was to win; if everything fell to pieces after crossing the finishing line it did not really matter very much; so far as the race was concerned it did not matter at all.

When assessing the irreplaceable part which Brooklands played in improving the breed it would be easy to allot excessive importance to the actual racing. Its primary purpose was to provide a novel form of entertainment for the general public, a purpose originally conceived from a financial motive. From a strictly technical point of view, all that racing did was to set targets and to provide the opportunity of proving and demonstrating that the technical measures taken had succeeded or failed; but only in the very short term. In this sense, the long term could be very long indeed; in relation to Brooklands it meant circling the track day after day, week after week. This was not the sort of activity calculated to entertain the public; neither was it particularly attractive or convenient from the point of view of the designer or his firm; yet, if he wanted to achieve reliability there was no alternative; neither was there any other place where such sustained high speed was possible.

THE YEARS OF RIVALRY

It was made apparent, during the years of rivalry between Sunbeam and Vauxhall, that success in racing and record breaking was not necessarily closely related to originality in engine design. The primary factor was meticulous attention to detail and that, taken to the limit, is as good a definition as can be found of the art of tuning. A striking example of what could be achieved by tuning was well demonstrated in another phase of rivalry in which Coatalen was involved – the contest between his newly designed 9-litre, 12-cylinder Sunbeam and the rather staid but highly tuned $4\frac{1}{2}$-litre, 4-cylinder Talbot. Neither engine embodied any of those advanced features which later would be recognised as indispensable for attainment of maximum ·power output. Both were side-valve engines. The Talbot was to all intents and purposes a standard model sufficiently mature to have been tuned to the limit; by virtue of its recent design the 12-cylinder Sunbeam was just a big engine, notwithstanding some originality in certain features of its design.

It was in February 1913 when Percy Lambert drove the Talbot an official distance of nearly 104 miles within the hour. The following October, Chassagne raised the record to nearly 108 miles with the 12-cylinder Sunbeam. It will be noted that the small margin of 4mph was out of proportion between two cars whose engine cylinder capacities were in the ratio of two to one. Whatever may have been the case with the Talbot, it seems very unlikely that the figure of 108 miles represented the best which the Sunbeam could do. Reliability of any engine diminishes as its peak power is approached; over a long distance a good driver will accordingly keep a good margin of performance in hand. In this matter Chassagne must have possessed a substantial advantage over Lambert who had no margin to spare. However, this was not the controlling factor; it was all a question of tyres and the risks the drivers were prepared to take. At this stage in their development the life of a tyre at 100mph was nothing more than a gamble; just how much of a gamble it was I was able to appreciate from personal observation.

During that October I happened to be at Brooklands trying out a new engine for my employers. When I arrived in the Paddock, I discovered that the

track was temporarily closed; it had been booked for consecutive record attempts by Lambert and Chassagne. A small gathering of Brooklands 'regulars' was assembled at the junction of the Finishing Straight and the Members' Banking, probably the fastest point along the course, it being situated on the one in twenty-five decline which led down to the Railway Straight. The obvious thing was to join them. Both the competing cars were there, each receiving last minute attention from a group of mechanics; Lambert and Chassagne were in conversation. At a signal from time-keeper Ebblewhite, everybody drew back to his chosen vantage point while Chassagne climbed into his Sunbeam. Very soon he was away, leaving a faint trail of blue smoke behind.

About a minute and a half later, he could be heard coming round behind the Members' Hill; in a flash he went by, high up on the banking and probably travelling at a good 115mph. Viewed from less than the full width of the track, the speed was really impressive; the effect was accentuated by the way the car swayed slightly from side to side, the driver visibly bouncing in his

Record–breaking in progress with a 1912 Sunbeam. The scene is at the junction of the Finishing-Straight and the Members' Banking

seat. This was only the first lap, with another thirty-six to go; it was a searching thought. So, with perfect regularity he came round again and again; at this rate he would break his own record easily. Then, after perhaps nine or ten laps and when he was practically opposite where we stood, there came a loud report as his off-side tyre burst. Simultaneously, the car swerved from the banking. Just when it seemed that nothing could prevent it from shooting over the inner edge of the track, the driver regained control and after an alarming series of twists and turns brought it safely to a stop some distance along the Railway Straight. Meanwhile, the Clerk of the Course had set out in the black and yellow staff-car to render assistance. He was soon back with Chassagne sitting beside him, shaken but unhurt.

Chassagne was an attractive personality; despite his unpleasant experience his faced was wreathed with smiles in response to congratulations

BROOKLANDS AUTOMOBILE RACING CLUB.

OFFICIAL RACE CARD.

PRICE SIXPENCE.

MONDAY, AUGUST 4th, 1913

1913 Race Programme cover

THE FIRST CAR IN THE WORLD TO ACHIEVE THE OFT - ATTEMPTED 100 - MILES - IN - ONE - HOUR RUN

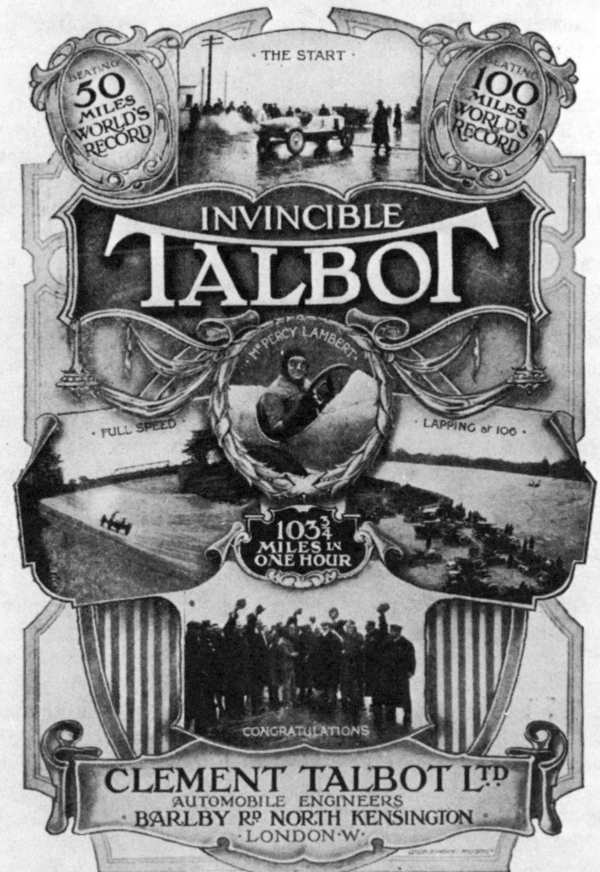

We have published a 40-page SOUVENIR ALBUM commemorating this historic feat————— beautifully produced in colours with over 100 illustrations————— A presentation copy will be forwarded to any reader of " Aeronautics " on request

Advertisement announcing 100 miles in the hour

on his fortunate escape. All he could say was 'It is nothing'! But it might very well have been otherwise, as he knew quite well. The whole episode could not have been very encouraging to Lambert whose turn to use the track had come. The small band of spectators expected his attempt to be postponed, but no: after a brief consultation with his supporters he walked over to the Talbot and climbed in. After wishing him luck, Chassagne walked away to the Paddock and its Club House where, no doubt, he found some refreshment suited to the occasion. As the Talbot's engine was run up, there could be detected among the spectators a certain tenseness which had been absent from the earlier start. The same thought was present in everybody's mind – would Lambert's tyres last the hour?

There followed the same sequence of events; the roar from the engine, the trail of blue smoke and the car disappearing into the distance. After the same lapse of time and travelling at much about the same speed, the Talbot came out from behind the hill, passing a little higher up the banking. One lap, two laps and maybe a third; then, just as the car was nearly due to appear, there came from behind the Members' Hill the frightening bang of a bursting tyre. As the Talbot came into sight it was slowing down sharply in a sequence of rather terrifying skids. It came to rest, still the right way up, almost where we stood. Again, it was the off-side rear tyre which had burst and what remained of it was wrapped around the rear axle, thus locking the wheel. A few days later and at practically the same point on the banking, an almost identical series of events, was to be repeated but this time with tragic results: the car overturned and Lambert was killed.

Both cars had been fitted with the then famous Palmer Cord tyres, widely accepted as the best obtainable. Sometimes they did last for a good deal more than an hour at 100mph; more often they did not. Unfortunately there was no means of knowing in advance whether they would or would not. What then, was the use of a 9-litre engines if tyres prevented it from doing much more than one of $4\frac{1}{2}$ litres? The answer was that the installation in a racing car of the 12-cylinder Sunbeam was merely incidental to Coatalen's first attempt to produce a higher powered engine than any yet available for aeroplanes; it was safer to do the initial running on four wheels rather than in an aircraft where engine failure could mean disaster. Thirty years later such initial testing would be done in the air on a flying test-bed; that is to say a standard type of aeroplane with its own power plant and not dependant upon the test engine for its flying. Aircraft big enough and stable enough for the purpose did not exist in 1913. Over and above these considerations was the fact that Coatalen enjoyed providing surprises for the motor racing fraternity. Soon after the war he would invert the process by designing a special chassis to accommodate one of his later types of aero-engines after it had seen much service in the air; it was to prove sensational in many different ways.

The morning of that October day had been made memorable enough by the abortive record breaking attempts; further insight into life at Brooklands may be gained by describing some of the events which enlivened the afternoon, when the track was again open for general use. The experimental JAP twin-cylinder engine that I was testing installed in a Royal Enfield combination, the sidecar of which was useful for carrying tools and spare parts so frequently needed. On this particular occasion the sidecar was occupied by a young mechanic who had never seen Brooklands and was anxious to make its acquaintance. As soon as the barriers had been removed we set out on a few circuits.

The Royal Enfield two-speed gear depended upon alternative use of two short chains from the engine to a countershaft which carried a pair of selective clutches; a third chain drove the rear wheel. The arrangement was one which greatly facilitated the use of the gear-change as a powerful brake; this, however, entailed abnormal inertia loads on the engine and it was the effects of these which were under investigation. To have carried out these experiments on the public highway would have been both impracticable and quite unacceptable to other road users. The tests would clearly be most effective if carried out on the fastest part of the track, which meant the vicinity of the morning's tyre failures. Consequently, when the first downward gear change was accompanied by a loud bang, it could well have been supposed to be the result of a burst tyre except for material evidence to the contrary. From somewhere low down between cycle and sidecar there flew upwards into the air an elongated object which, in the early course of its flight, tore a slit in the right-hand sleeve of my passenger's coat. It was the racing of the engine which revealed that the flying object was one of the front chains. To have walked about the track looking for it, would have been a serious breach of regulations; the only thing to do was to continue the circuit in the one operative gear and report the presence of the potential source of danger.

The further we went, the more erratic became the running of the engine; all the symptoms suggested a flooding carburettor. On arrival in the Paddock, the passenger still reclining in the sidecar, the float-chamber promptly burst into flames. With a rapidity which was scarcely believable, a man in a peaked cap was on the scene with a fire extinguisher and put out the fire. Inspection showed that the flying chain had hit the float-chamber which, being free to swivel, had been pressed hard against the hot fins of one engine cylinder thus causing the petrol eventually to boil. As might be imagined, by this time my passenger was in a highly nervous condition. There was more to come. While I was engaged in fitting a spare chain, I heard the sound of an aeroplane taking off near the aero-sheds on the far side of the track. These were the days when such an event excited everybody's attention; one never knew what might happen.

The machine happened to be the first Sopwith Tabloid, a small biplane which made history; the pilot was Harry Hawker. Something was obviously amiss with the engine, the cylinders firing in a most irregular manner. When still at little more than a couple of hundred feet, it spluttered and stopped; the plane stalled and then spun cartwheel fashion down into trees just outside the track. The noise which accompanied the impact was louder than the tyre-bursts of the morning and was followed by the breaking of boughs and branches. Everybody rushed from the Paddock to render assistance. I would have joined them but for the pleading of my passenger who by now had had enough. Upon hearing that Hawker was safe, we set off home in the gathering darkness. Upon arrival, my passenger insisted that for the latter part of the journey he could see flames lapping the edge of the float-chamber. For my part, I never believed it. So ended what could well rank as a typical day at Brooklands.

It is very doubtful whether even downhill this Royal Enfield combination was capable of a mile a minute. The shape of the handlebars compelled an upright position productive of much air-resistance; likewise the sidecar body which was a cross between a coffin and a bath-chair. Steering and stability were uncertain, especially when a heavy cross-wind was blowing. Soon after the First World War, when a low built chassis carried a streamlined body of minimum cross-section, sidecar speeds rose towards 80mph and a special technique had to be acquired in their handling. Provided the front fork structure possessed sufficient transverse stiffness and carried a friction-damper to prevent synchronous oscillation of the front wheel, things were not too difficult except that the bumps

Above : Lanchester driven by Lionel Rapson
Below : The ill-fated Percy Lambert and his record-breaking Talbot

and ruts made riding physically arduous. These are matters which can best be appreciated against the wider background of motor-cycle racing in general.

The part played by motor-cycle racing in the story of Brooklands must not be underestimated. For many, it was the gateway to car racing and flying. Although they were three separate and distinctive forms of activity, with the one reacting against the other two, they all had much in common. Race meetings apart, one could not spend much time at the track without making close acquaintance with speed enthusiasts of every type. There was possibly one distinction; the only people likely to have much money to spare were the people who raced cars. Except for those favoured by some appropriate association with the motor industry, car racing was the preserve of the relatively well to do; whereas, for the sum of fifty pounds could be bought one of several makes of motor-cycle which would offer the purchaser the chance of moderate success in racing.

For quite a small supplementary payment it was possible to buy a 3½hp (500cc) Norton certified by the track authorities as having attained a speed of 70mph. The sale of these special 'speed models' was sufficient to warrant the permanent residence at Brooklands of the leading Norton rider, by name O'Donovan. He was among that number who could improve considerably the performance of any production engine merely by dismantling, refitting the mating parts and reassembling the engine. O'Donovan was widely credited with possessing 'secrets of tune' although he never made the claim himself; he was first and foremost a first-class engineering fitter with an intuitive understanding of the petrol engine and a first class rider as well.

The Tourist Trophy Races held annually in the Isle of Man exerted upon the development of the motor-cycle an influence far exceeding anything which the equivalent spasmodic events exercised on car design. Every manufacturer who competed or had ever competed in these races marketed a 'TT' model which, for the most part, was faster than the standard touring model. These were the machines which the amateur would ride at Brooklands. There was no equivalent in the world of cars. The motor-cycle industry made wider use of proprietary engines, in particular JAP engines produced by the firm founded by J A Prestwich, with whom I served a term. It was with a JAP motor-cycle engine that A V Roe, the first man to fly in Great Britain, conducted his initial experiments. At first, he was only able to taxi his machine and did not actually fly until he was able to borrow an Antoinette aero-engine. When the time arrived to return the Antoinette to the lender, he succeeded in flying with the 9hp JAP.

Prestwich first attracted notice by producing 3-cylinder air-cooled engines of the 'broad arrow' type (so named from the relative disposition of the cylinders) used in the pacemaking machines of the pedal-cycle boarded race tracks. So strong was the demand for his single and twin cylinder engines that more attention was devoted to economy of production than to technical advance. J A Prestwich was a clever and able man who, had he directed his whole energies to engine development, would have achieved great things. As it was, he pursued a number of divergent interests; at the time that I knew him, he was deeply involved in the design and construction of cinematic apparatus.

For a time, most of the successful racing motor-cycles were fitted with JAP engines, notably the Matchless machines already mentioned. It was only in the most powerful class (the 1,000cc twins) that they continued to hold their own, even against the onslaught of the Indians and Harley-Davidsons from America. In the single cylinder classes (250, 350 and 500cc) they were to be outpaced by the Nortons, Triumphs, Rudge-Whitworths and several more besides. These

O'Donovan astride his Norton

makers incorporated engines of their own design and found it worthwhile to pursue an increasing standard of performance for the sake of the advertising value attendant upon racing successes.

The whole circumstances attaching to motor-cycle racing differed widely from those of the racing car; manufacturers' competition activities were directed predominantly towards the Isle of Man. Brooklands made great contributions to progress, not so much through direct participation by the 'trade' as through the disinterested devotion of a number of dedicated amateurs who, working all day long in their rented sheds in the Paddock, had no object in life except to obtain a few more mph. This unique and dedicated band went unrecorded and unsung; they vanished with the outbreak of war in 1914 and few, if any, survived service in the armed forces.

One who is particularly remembered was a Cambridge graduate who was just able to live and race on the interest from a small legacy which he had inherited. He possessed two machines the makes of which are now forgotten except that both were fitted with OHV JAP engines. In spite of all his efforts he could never maintain with either of them their maximum speed long enough to win a race. He temporarily abandoned actual racing until he could discover the technical reasons accounting for a marked loss of speed which invariably occurred as soon as the engine had become really hot. By persistent labour and experiment, aided by his academic training, he eventually solved the problem. He proved and could demonstrate that, when really hot, the bolted on valve-chest distorted out of alignment with the valve-seatings. Knowing that I had some connection with the makers he sought my personal advocacy of his findings which he had disclosed to the firm by letter. The fact that his evidence fell on deaf ears in no way detracts from the value of his work, even though it was to bear fruit in a field which he could not have foreseen. In similar ways, his colleagues were also instrumental in aiding the development of the petrol engine.

In those times, when so much of motor engineering proceeded on a basis of rule of thumb and personal prejudice, Brooklands could fairly be described as the development department of the industry. It served to develop not only the product but, more far reaching, the men who later would be in positions of authority. Notable among them was W O Bentley who, before going on to design and manufacture Bentley cars, was to perfect the rotary aero-engine in the design of his BR1 and BR2 engines famous in the First World War: he raced a Rex motor-cycle at Brooklands in 1909. Then, soon after that war, F B Halford appeared on the track, who went on to design the Napier Sabre and a series of De Havilland jet engines; prior to his success with the Halford Special racing car, he had won races and broken records on the four-valve Triumph motor-cycle.

It was impossible to become involved with Brooklands and then forget all about it; one way or another it always left its mark and this might manifest itself in many different ways. If one went to watch the racing, one wanted to go again; in the same way, to race once was to want to race again. Yet both these things were simple reactions not to be compared with more subtle consequences of deeper involvement for, thereby, one was tacitly admitted into an otherwise closed fraternity in which money and social distinctions had no meaning. It was the resultant 'atmosphere' which gave to Brooklands a claim to be a place of education through the ready interchange of thought and experience. In effect, everybody was trying to solve a series of problems; individually the problems might be very different though the ultimate aim of all was the same. If you like, it may be said we picked each other's brains, but only in the aid of a common cause.

DIMINISHING RETURNS

If the progress in speeds of cars and motor-cycles is examined respectively over the whole life of Brooklands, they will be found to follow entirely different patterns. The exact speeds attained during the first few months are the subject of some uncertainty, although there is little doubt that 100mph was exceeded on a number of occasions. It is quite certain that Newton was timed during 1908 at practically 120mph; at this time very few motor-cycles were capable of exceeding 60mph. From such figures it will be evident that, from a spectacular point of view, motor-cycles were just not in the running; in consequence, there was a marked difference in the types of crowd attracted to the two forms of racing. In fact, so far as motor-cycle race meetings were concerned the word 'crowd' would have been something of a misnomer. In addition to being much smaller in number, spectators were inspired by different motives. They did not come in expectation of being thrilled; they were much more interested in technical detail, while a large number of them hoped one day to be competitors.

The steady pursuit of increasing power output from unit cylinder capacity went on in connection with both types of vehicle. In the case of motor-cycles it was seen to be happening and formed a primary source of interest; among the racing cars the process was obscured by the performances of the monsters. At no time were there ever any 'monster' motor-cycles; they disappeared with the boarded cycle tracks. It would also be fair to say that the design of racing motor-cycles remained static; their speeds increased over the years by continual refinements in the art of tuning and the adoption of special fuels which permitted of much higher compression-ratios.

The stagnation in design was due to a number of factors. In the first place, the proprietary engine manufacturers were conservative to a degree; they could sell their engines anyway, so why bother? Then, again, the lower income brackets from which amateur riders tended to be drawn did not provide the financial resources necessary for building novel designs on a basis of private venture. Right from the early days there were always to be

found both riders and spectators at motor-cycle meetings who had clever ideas or had even completed designs which could have lifted the whole scale of performance to greater heights. Unable to find firms or private individuals willing to back them, they transferred their ingenuity to other fields.

There were also some very practical considerations of a technical nature which hindered development of the racing motor-cycle. The requirements of stability and control severely curtailed acceptable limits of wheelbase, height and weight. There was very good reason for absence of an 'unlimited' class at race-meetings, for nothing of the kind was a practical proposition. The type of engine to be found in the largest recognised class, the 1,000cc twin fitted the conventional frame of normal wheelbase like a glove. It is true that specially designed engines of at least twice that cylinder capacity could have been accommodated within a wheelbase only a few inches longer, but the design of the rest of the machine would have made considerable demands upon the de-

Informal test of a works chassis

signer. The resultant cost of manufacture would have been regarded as prohibitive. Dwarfing all these problems would have been the improbability of transmitting in safety the increased power through a single tyre. A design study in depth concerning these matters led to such unconventional expedients as back-wheel steering and front-wheel drive among other novelties; even one of the wealthy oil companies balked at the combination of unorthodoxy and unforeseeable cost.

With the racing car the case was entirely different. To begin with, stability and control were attainable quite independently of size and weight of engine; although it is not to be implied that these desirable qualities were in fact always achieved. It was at least practically possible to take an existing chassis and, with little modification, substitute a different engine of much greater cylinder capacity than the original; it was not only possible, it was frequently done. The resultant motor cars may not always have

Charlie Collier – fastest rider of the time

proved particularly convenient or safe vehicles to drive, but there was never any lack of courageous drivers to drive them; if they should be so unfortunate as to go over the top of the banking or to disappear through the fencing on the Railway Straight it was simply regarded as the luck of the game. During the interim, their circling of the track would have afforded the spectators many a thrill, while the drivers would have experienced a sense of satisfying accomplishment so profound as to defy analysis. These comparative observations concerning racing cars and motor-cycles must not be allowed to pass without noting, in anticipation, that during 1938 a Brough Superior motor-cycle, supercharged yet still with only a 1,000cc twin JAP engine, was timed over the kilometre at 143mph, almost as fast as the officially timed speed of any car at Brooklands despite the advantage of an engine of several times that unit litre of cylinder capacity.

It is regrettable that comprehensive working drawings are not available of the giant cars which raced at the track in the early days; photographs alone can only indicate the general features, so that it is only in terms of generalities that the first and last cars can be compared. The high build and lack of streamlining has already been mentioned. Two other obvious differences are the increase of tyre cross-section and the disappearance (with few exceptions) of final chain-drive to the rear wheels. It remains remarkable how long a time elapsed before larger section tyres came into general use; even so, the bugbear of the bursting tyre remained to the very end. It is quite clear that through the whole life of Brooklands racing cars remained inadequately tyred; it is evidence in support of the opinion that, from the ordinary motorist's point of view, the value of Brooklands in improving the breed tended to decline with the passage of time. The reasons are not hard to understand.

Right until well into the 1950s it was distinctly exceptional to encounter on British roads a motor car travelling at much more than 45 or 50mph. At that sort of speed engines and tyres had become very reliable and the cars economical to run; moreover, this state of affairs had existed over the previous twenty or twenty-five years. It was the increasing mass of private users which constituted the market for cars and their component parts. The provision of special tyres for use at speeds around 100mph was therefore not a commercial proposition; those firms who sought to meet this highly specialised field did so as part of an experimental programme, always with one eye on the accompanying opportunities for advertisement. Likewise with the car as a whole. A few manufacturers found that a limited market existed for sports cars of higher performance than the normal touring or utility model. All the technical 'know-how' required to produce satisfactory models of this type (and their tyres) had already been gained through track-racing by the middle 1920s. It is in the light of these circumstances that the active life of Brooklands may be divided into three periods. Technically, Brook-

Champion Jake De Rosier

lands was a story of diminishing returns; as a spectacle it reached its zenith in its final years.

The first period lasted from the opening in 1907 to the outbreak of war in 1914. These were the crucial years which moulded the essence of the Brooklands tradition and laid the foundations of technical advance. During the war years, the fruits of the preceeding seven were to germinate not so much in better motor-cars as in a first generation of reliable aero-engines. (The aircraft apart from its engine has yet to come under review).

Start of an Essex Motor Cycle Club handicap race

Start of an Essex Motor Cycle Club handicap race

From 1920 to 1925 the track was open to all who cared to ride or drive or race. Then the extemporised artificial hazards were introduced, soon to be followed by additional track and mountain circuit. The old was giving place to the new and with it inevitably came an increasing predominance of the professional element. Improvement of the breed continued through channels less open to direct observation. The link between Coatalen's 9-litre Sunbeam and the aero-engines of the First World War was obvious; it would not be easy to unravel connections between Brooklands and the jet engines which came after the track's demise.

It would be impossible here to give much detail of the varied racing and nearly continuous record breaking which took place at Brooklands during that first period which terminated in 1914. Bearing in mind the six separate classes ranging in terms of RAC rating from 16 to 90hp in addition to the unclassified monsters, even a brief summary is impossible. The situation is further complicated by varying distances over which speed might be measured – half mile, kilometre, one mile, ten laps and so forth. However, the general trend towards increasing speed can be illustrated by just a few examples. In the 16hp class, over as short a time as 1910 to 1913 the flying half mile record was raised from 72-mph (Sunbeam) to 106mph (Peugeot). This increase of 34mph is quite remarkable, yet equally impressive are the figures of the ten-lap record for the 26hp rating between 1907 and 1913: 71mph (Napier) to 110mph (Talbot). As might be expected, the unclassified (ie unlimited) cars did not conform to quite the same pattern; $21\frac{1}{2}$-litre Benz was officially timed at 128mph in 1908, the same as the fastest speed to be recorded in 1914.

The progressive rise in speed which distinguished the lower powered classes reflects the increasing output being obtained from unit cylinder capacity; the cars were undoubtedly being driven to their limits. This is unlikely to have been the case where the really big cars were concerned. Speeds were limited by the indifferent road holding qualities of the vehicles on so rough a surface as well as by their drivers in the hope of extending the life of the tyres; in this matter judgement and discipline could be critical. During the last period of

H D Davidson on the saddle of a flat-twin Harley. (No connection with Harley-Davidson)

Brooklands, speeds in the neighbourhood of 140mph would cease to be exceptional, not only as the consequence of improvement in the breed of motor-car but equally through perfection of driving techniques on the part of an élite handful of drivers. At any time during the life of the track it was open to any driver so inclined to take a chance by riding near the lip of the banking: but to hold consistently a course within inches of the edge, lap after lap, required a mastery beyond the reach of those early drivers who were, so to speak, feeling their way in an unfamiliar environment.

Not all the early cars were capable of breaking records within their respective classes, neither did every car necessarily show its best paces in every race for which it was entered. Engines could be temperamental and have their 'off days'; so could their drivers. Then there had to be considered the system of handicapping. Cars and drivers would be handicapped according to their previously observed performance; a driver might therefore find it expedient to 'go slow' for a period in the hope of improving his handicap on a later occasion. The object of handicap races was to provide a close and exciting finish for the benefit of the spectators. During the early years it was not uncommon for the proceedings to be enlivened by the entry of competitors who from the beginning had no chance of even obtaining a place; as they straggled home, long after all the others had crossed the finishing line, their safe arrival would be greeted with a round of ironic applause. It was therefore by no means unusual for a car travelling high on the banking to pass others hugging the inside-edge at half their speed. It was all part of the variety of life to be found at Brooklands.

Another source of special interest was the occasional challenge which would be made by one owner or driver to another. The stakes might be anything from a few sovereigns to a hundred or more. Among the earliest of these occasions was when S F Edge offered stakes of a thousand pounds, later raised to ten times the amount; it was never taken up. It need hardly be said that this kind of prodigality was confined to the car racing fraternity; motor-cyclists raced only for cups and medals. There was, however, one notable exception when, in 1911, a challenge came from America. From time to time the motor-cycling press had published reports of racing as carried on in the United States where, from all accounts, general conditions bore no resemblance to anything known in this country. Racing on 'dirt-tracks' appeared to be very popular; otherwise riders competed on the kind of boarded track which here had long since been abandoned. It further appeared that both forms of racing were accompanied by very questionable practices; among them the mixing of picric acid with the petrol in order to render exhaust gases so revolting as to discourage overtaking by a faster rider. It was against this background that there was received a challenge on behalf of a champion rider of the name Jake de Rosier. He proposed to bring his 1,000cc twin-cylinder Indian to England where he would be prepared to meet, and beat, any rider who might be nominated.

Easily our fastest rider at that time was C R Collier on his 1,000cc twin Matchless; it was accordingly arranged that he should meet de Rosier at Brooklands in a rubber of three races. Collier's current best speed was in the higher eighties, whereas the American was credited with having exceeded 90mph. It looked like being very close match. Meanwhile, the arrival of the American champion was awaited with a certain measure of apprehension; nobody could forget about the picric acid. In the event, de Rosier was found to be a good sports man and made a very pleasing impression; with that aptness for concise and pungent phrase for which his countrymen are noted, he was to concede that riding round Brooklands

at 90mph was 'no tea-party'; nevertheless, he won.

The two deciding races had been won at just over the level 90mph, a speed which Collier could not quite reach. Although a good loser when the occasion demanded, he was not accustomed to being in that position. He could not rest until he had been officially timed at something in excess of this now mystical figure; all the resources of his firm were diverted to

1,000 cc Zenith JAP with specially-designed racing side-car. P Brewster in the saddle after a win at 88mph in July 1927

this end. It was not very long before he succeeded in his aim although with only a small margin. Soon afterwards, he decided to retire from racing and to concentrate on problems of production. His retirement marked the close of a definite phase of motor-cycle racing.

Above: More wicker bodywork, with 1,000 cc Zenith JAP. F W Barnes in the saddle. Below: 1,000 cc Brough Superior (supercharged). Baragwanath in the saddle

Above: C F Temple with his 1,000 cc British Anzani engine in a modified Harley-Davidson frame **Below:** 1,000 cc side-valve twin cylinder Brough Superior. Watson Bourne in the saddle; George Brough standing

By no means all effort at Brooklands was directed towards progressive increase of speed; there were occasions when a manufacturer would make use of the track for some particular demonstration where the quality of reliability would assume considerably greater importance than mere speed. A prominent example was the extended running, in 1909, of two Daimler cars fitted with the recently adopted double-sleeve-valve type of engine known as the 'Silent Knight' in recognition of its inventor. Two cars, of different hp ratings, were driven a distance exceeding by 400 miles that covered by the three Napier cars two years earlier. The fact that the two Daimlers averaged only 42mph is evidence that the purpose of the runs was to demonstrate reliability. No real effort was ever made to attain a higher power output per unit of cylinder capacity, the sole aim being to combine moderate performance with silence of operation; on this foundation they sought to establish an exclusive clientele who could afford to pay for the highest standard of luxury. It was a field where competition was at a minimum; the Napier-Edge consortium was too preoccupied with speed to do more than dabble in this specialised market, while Rolls-Royce were planning at deeper level a policy which would require a much longer time to reach its full fruition. From a technical point of view, the rise and fall of the double-sleeve-valve engine is an instructive example of obsolescent ingenuity.

For a number of years, the typical motor-car engine was to remain noisy in its operation, the noise largely deriving from the poppet-valve and its associated mechanism; the pursuit of greater output from unit cylinder capacity encouraged development of valve-gear productive of ever higher levels of noise. C Y Knight completely eliminated this noise at its source by substituting for poppet-valves his system of double sleeves which reciprocated within the cylinder thus avoiding any violent impact between metallic surfaces. By its very nature it was a costly form of construction, a disadvantage aggravated by the existing stage of machine tool development. It is very doubtful whether the engine on its own could ever have formed the basis of a successful commercial venture. The Daimler company did not take the risk. Instead, they piled on the luxury by the supplementary additions of magnificent upholstery and silver-plating throughout; they then enclosed the total collection in coachwork so massive as to symbolize the opulence of the purchaser. What Knight had overlooked was that, once engine designers found time to embark upon the study and analysis of conventional valve-gears, the way would be found to render the poppet-valve mechanism as quiet as the sleeve and without additional cost. The Knight engine long survived its technical supercession only through having earlier attained pre-eminence as an indispensable insignia of royalty.

What is not so easily explained is the rise and fall of the first single-sleeve-valve engine which, after a meteoric appearance as a record breaker at Brooklands, disappeared into obscurity until revival of the type many years later as the ultimate form of piston type aero-engine. Early in 1913 there was brought to the track an Argyll car incorporating a single-sleeve-valve engine which not only proved the equal of the Silent Knight in terms of reliability over long distances, but also travelled at practically twice the speed. Yet kings and queens were to travel about in their massive Daimlers for years after the single-sleeve engine had gone into temporary oblivion. It is one of the mysteries of engineering, only to be unravelled by deep enquiry into the chequered history of machine-tool development in relation to engine manufacture; a subject clearly beyond the scope of these pages. No less involved was the obstinate refusal of all but a tiny minority of the buying

Tudor and Thompson in Douglas combination with wicker bodywork

public to support any marked departure from prevailing fashions in motorcars; Brooklands was about the only place where such fashions held no sway

However, with all its diverse enterprise and unattachment to preconceived ideas, Brooklands (or rather its first Clerk of Course) stumbled badly at its first acquaintance with the aeroplane. Those persons more mystically inclined may detect the working of an inscrutable justice whereby an initially unwelcome intruder came eventually to accomplish a takeover whereby both racing car and motor-cycle were to be driven from their spiritual home.

FLYING COLONY

The circumstances surrounding the offer, made by the Brooklands authorities soon after opening day, to award a prize of £2,500 for the first flight of an aeroplane round a complete circuit of the track, are somewhat uncertain. It has been suggested that the sole object was to gain cheap publicity. No one had yet flown a self-propelled 'heavier than air' machine in the British Isles and the great majority of people saw no prospect of anybody succeeding in the future, still less by the end of the year as was stipulated in the announcement. This would seem too cynical a view for, whatever may have been the opinion of the great majority, inclusive perhaps of those members of the BARC committee obsessed with the psychology of horse racing, there was among the committee a number of technically well informed men; not everybody doubted the reports of Wilbur Wright having flown in 1903. Whatever may have been the motive underlying the offer, there came a quick response when, in September 1907, A V Roe arrived at Brooklands seeking per-

mission to build a shed in which he proposed to build an aeroplane. In, around and about this shed was to be sustained an epic struggle against disappointment, frustration, ignorant interference and ill will; it is the one black page in the history of the track.

The story of A V Roe's unrelenting persistence in his efforts to build and fly his aeroplane is to be found in his all too brief autobiography. The source of all his avoidable troubles was the first Clerk of the Course E Rodakowski, who apparently had little time for Roe. The BARC had issued a general invitation to prospective aviators to 'exercise' their machines on the track; Rodakowski seemed more interested in pushing them out. Roe said of him that his principal asset was a voice of phenomenal penetrative power and that when he whispered in the Paddock it could be heard on the Byfleet Banking a mile away.

In relation to the financial and material resources required for his purposes, Roe by comparison was far poorer than any who have ever contended for success at Brooklands.

In his shed he lived on a diet of dates and kippers and spent the nights sleeping in a wooden crate. Proposing at one time to build one of his aeroplanes in steel tube, he was compelled to revert to wood through sheer lack of money. For similar reasons, the wings of his early machines were covered by oiled brown-paper and on this precarious substitute he made many of his early flights. During his first sojourn at Brooklands, until his first flight, Roe must have been a very lonely man; he records that for days at a time his only visitor was a robin. Car drivers when called upon were pleased to assist by towing his machine along the Finishing Straight, but their enthusiasm was not matched by their judgement, thus frequently putting his life in danger. At intervals, Rodakowski would insist that the shed be moved to a different position, on one occasion to the other side of some high railings. When, in June 1908, Roe eventually succeeded in flying, the flight was witnessed only by a couple of workmen; an unfortunate circumstance which delayed the full recognition

**Lone aviator A V Roe in his wor	kshed, 1908**

which the momentous event deserved. No sooner had Roe become the first man to fly in England than Rodakowski gave him peremptory instructions to depart from Brooklands. Similar instructions had been given before and ignored; this time there was no alternative but submission. Unable to transport the shed, Roe had to sell it to his persecutor for a mere pittance; taking his aeroplane with him he went into exile on the Lea Valley Marshes, there to set up his workshop and hangar in a couple of railway arches. More than a year later, he was to return.

It might seem incomprehensible that A V Roe should have suffered such abominable treatment in a place later to become renowned as the very embodiment of friendliness, mutual help and goodwill. The explanation is that Brooklands, the real Brooklands, remained largely sterile until the appointment in 1909 of Major Lindsay Lloyd as Clerk of the Course. He soon arranged for an area near the Byfleet

Above : A V Roe's machine leaves the shed. Below : A V Roe inspects his crashed triplane, 1909

Banking to be cleared so that aeroplanes could take off (when they were able) and land; here sheds and hangars began to be erected for their housing, maintenance and even manufacture. Among the first to take advantage of these facilities was Roe himself. Here he continued to fly his famous triplanes and to build biplanes which followed. He also opened a flying school and taught others to fly. He soon began to receive an occasional order or two and thus found it necessary to delegate the running of the flying-school. One by one, he increased his workshop staff though constantly in difficulty to make ends meet until, with the accession of his brother who was able to bring further capital, there were laid the initial foundations of a firm which, during the First World War, would manufacture aircraft by the thousand. It is tempting to wonder what Rodakowski thought of it all.

These first few aero-sheds, as they were called, rapidly increased in number until eventually there were

Clearing a site for the aviation section, 1909

forty or more of them; their number grew as there arrived, from near and far, what was perhaps the most amazing colony of remarkable men (some of them little more than boys) that has ever before or since gathered together in so small a space, every one of them utterly dedicated to an ambition to fly. Some just wanted to learn to fly, and having learned, to keep on flying. Others, like Roe, were more seriously inclined and inspired with ideas for the design and construction of better and better aeroplanes. Some came with money to pay for their tuition wherever they could get it; others sought jobs with very little pay or even with no pay at all and worked their way to qualify for a 'flying ticket'. A few who had the necessary money bought an aeroplane and taught themselves to fly. By no means all of them were just high-spirited youngsters obsessed with the simple ambition of becoming an

aviator; many were engineers of some experience attracted by the novel problems which the aeroplane presented. Among this infinitely variegated body of inspired men, each one individualistic to the last degree, were to be revealed a few 'natural' flyers; these men were complete masters of the art from the beginning. Some of them would go on to become idols of an adoring public who would come in tens of thousands to watch their aerobatics at Hendon and elsewhere; the others, in self-effacing solitude remote from admiring crowds, would daily accept incalculable risks in the testing of unproven aeroplanes and engage in perilous experiments in search of knowledge on which others would build.

In both types of career the average

Flying simulators are nothing new. The general public get their chance to experience the effect of flying in this Eardly Billing oscillator

expectation of life was minimal; time and again, a meteoric rise to fame would end in sudden tragedy. Within a very few years, whole generations would meet their deaths just as suddenly in war, but the thing had not happened yet. The continuing succession of aeroplane crashes produced a disproportionate effect upon a public beguiled by the illusion of perpetual peace and safety. As a result, the pioneers of aviation became invested with an unprecedented glamour of which they themselves remained unconscious. For these matters to be placed in better perspective it is necessary to see the stage through the

Activity outside and above the Blue Bird restaurant

9
8
THE BLUE BIRD RESTAURANT.
LUNCHEONS, TEAS
& REFRESHMENTS AT POPULAR PRICES

Hubert Latham with his Antoinette and Gordon Watney with a 60hp Mercedes decide to race each other, June 1911

eyes of those who played their parts upon it.

Innumerable hazards of early aviation were cheerfully accepted because they were thought to be unavoidable. Every machine was an experiment, its design based largely on ignorance; factual knowledge could only be gained by a process of trial and error, a process inevitably expensive in life and limb. Practically every aeroplane was unstable in all directions and none of their pilots expected them to be otherwise; to most of them the idea of a stable machine was just an unattainable dream. Even in their overall shape and means of control few machines were quite alike. Elevators and rubber were alternately in front or behind; flexing wings were found in one machine, ailerons in another; one, two or even three propellers operated in front or pushed from behind; above all, these were engines liable at any moment to falter and splutter to a stop, engines grossly underpowered for the job they were doing. Anyone inclined to worry too much about these things would simply have stayed on the ground. Then there were the inadequacies of detail construction.

It is disturbing to recall, sixty years

Mercedes and Antoinette during the duel

later, some of the mechnical improvisations to be seen during a stroll round
the aero-sheds. Pieces of wire, cord
and canvas, lengths of bamboo and
even the domestic broomstick were
pressed into the most unlikely service.
In contrast, there were machines
embodying workmanship of the highest order. Yet to what end if stresses
had not been calculated through want
of the necessary data? Besides, what
was known with certainty in those days
of the tensile-strength or elastic-
modulus of oak, spruce or ash?

In its initial stages, flying was pre-

In takeoff, as in landing, there loomed
large among the minor perils of flight
the ever present risk of involuntary
descent into the sewage farm which
lay adjacent to the flying ground; but
there were few early pilots who had
never found their way into the repul-
sive muck. For those who did, the stuff
was soft and yielding; immersion could
be infinitely preferable to forceful
impact with solid earth. Perhaps it was
for this very reason that the sewage
farm was credited with an active spirit
of malevolence and magnetic attraction
contrary to all common sense. These

**Latham's Antoinette monoplane
makes a crash landing on the
Martin Handasyde hangar—Whit
Monday 1911**

carious enough without the additional
complications of a strong breeze:
stillness of the air was considered
essential. This was a condition most
likely to occur soon after dawn and
this encouraged the practice of sleeping on the premises. Simple methods
were employed for confirming the
stillness of the atmosphere; dropping
a feather at arm's length or watching
the ascent of smoke from a cigarette.
With the low powered engines, takeoff
was a very uncertain business; the
increased lift from a head-wind could
make all the difference.

and other superstitions were among
the lighter topics of conversation at the
Blue Bird Restaurant where everybody
who worked in the adjacent hangars
and sheds foregathered for food and
relaxation. Members of the racing-car
and motor-cycle fraternity were among
its patrons although for the most part
they favoured the club house in the
Paddock.

BROOKLANDS
AVIATION LTD
SCHOOL of FLYING

Machines of the Deperdussin Flying School, 1912

The concrete perimeter and the flying ground within its bounds represented two different ways of life; day to day necessities did not compel active co-operation; the strongest bond between them was a mutual interest in the vagaries of the internal combustion engine. The closest links were through those pilots and instructors who also participated in racing on the track. Particularly remembered among these was Gordon Bell, a 'natural' flyer if ever there was one. On his very first flight he succeeded in extricating his machine from a dangerous situation with only seconds to spare from total disaster. He was credited with having flown practically every type of aeroplane that was capable of being flown; by way of relaxation he raced a twin-cylinder BAT JAP motor-cycle and it was in this way that I came to make his acquaintance.

The necessity of wearing spectacles must have been very irksome to one of so intrepid a disposition, but he made light of it as he did the impediment in his speech; he was gifted with an individual brand of dry humour which enabled him to surmount the most improbable difficulties; and underlying it all was a depth of technical appreciation and understanding that was quite exceptional. He survived a number of crashes, one of which was almost-fatal, only to lose his life in 1918 through one of those accidents which never should have happened. In some measure, these qualities were characteristic of those who pioneered the art of flying. In order that a due sense of proportion may be preserved, it should be pointed out that not all these early pilots came to an untimely end; happily, some still survive.

It was the flights of Wilbur Wright during his first visit to France during 1908 which brought the British public to recognise that the aeroplane had become an accomplished fact; it required the crossing of the English Channel by Bleriot during the following year to bring full realisation that, in the journalist's phrase, 'England was no longer an island'. It was another Bleriot monoplane which finally put Brooklands 'on the map'. In 1913, Pégout came to give his exhibitions of 'looping the loop'. Record crowds paid for admission and thousands more watched the flying from outside. Brooklands had really arrived, although not in quite the manner which its founders had foreseen.

It is doubtful how far there followed increased attendance at race-meetings. The racing-car had now found a rival, and aeroplane races were organised, enjoying the additional advantage of novelty. However, in the new field of entertainment Brooklands itself was faced with increasing competition from a rival attraction – flying-meetings every week-end at Hendon aerodrome, a site closer to the centre of London. It is idle to speculate how this competition might have been resolved for, within a few months, there came the outbreak of war and both aerodromes were taken over for military purposes. It would be nearly six years before motor racing returned to Brooklands; meanwhile aviation was to pass from the state of infancy and become the third arm of the defence forces.

So ended the first period in the life of Brooklands. If an undue proportion of space should seem to have been devoted to this period at the expense of the other two, there are good reasons to account for it. This initial stage, from 1907 to 1914, was the crucial one; it established the essential tradition which would permeate the remaining life of the track. Seeds had been sown which would germinate during the war and burst into full flower between 1920 and 1925. Thereafter would occur a subtle change. Brooklands motor racing as a spectacle would be vastly improved, though its continuing contribution to improvement of the breed would become a matter of opinion.

View of the aviation centre, 1932

FREE FOR ALL

When the re-opening of Brooklands was announced, early in 1920, everyone was greatly concerned to know in what condition they would find the track after the long occuption of the aerodrome by the (now) Royal Air Force. A certain amount of damage by transit of heavy lorries with solid tyres was to be expected; more serious might be the normal ravages of frost and weather, accentuated by absence of regular maintenance. First impressions upon arrival for the opening race-meeting were not reassuring; it had been raining for the previous twenty-four hours and the flat parts of the track carried great sheets of water. from which it might be deduced that a certain amount of subsidence had occurred.

The Paddock was crowded as it had rarely ever been crowded before with racing cars, motor-cycles and competitors; inside the club house, the committee was deciding whether or not the meeting should be abandoned or postponed. Now and then, an engine would be started and a car driven through the gate to the Finishing Straight, sending up showers of water from the back wheels and drenching everybody within range. Once out on the circuit, the car became practically invisible in a cloud of spray and was soon back in the Paddock with both driver and mechanic drenched to the skin. It all looked very unpromising. It was finally decided to postpone the meeting until the following week. Despite the inclement weather, the crowd was slow to disperse; chiefly because there were so many opportunities to meet old friends. A principal subject of conversation was the unexpectedly large attendance.

Among the innumerable and far reaching changes brought about by the war had been the enormous increase in the number of people brought into personal contact with the motor-vehicle and the internal combustion engine – aircraft pilots, motor-cycle dispatch-riders, drivers of tanks, military cars and lorries, not to mention all those who had been concerned with repair and maintenance; it could not be surprising if some of them had become inspired with the idea of

Disappointment in the Paddock. Rain compels postponement of racing

motor-racing, especially when a cash gratuity on discharge could provide the capital for indulging their new-found interest. It needed only a tiny proportion visibly to swell the ranks at Brooklands. Parallel with this development many managements, faced by sudden cancellations of war contracts, were seeking new markets for their greatly augmented production capacity, and the motor industry had become an obvious choice. New models having been designed and built were in need of advertisement; what better means than racing ?

Similarly, manufacturers of petrol, oil, tyres and other accessories were equally in need of advertisement to re-establish retail sales, for which purpose they were prepared to pay generous bonuses to winners and breakers of records. In these various ways, it became possible for people to drive and ride at Brooklands who before the war could not have faced the expense even had the opportunity been available.

There were also those 'old hands' who had survived the war and im-patiently awaited the chance to resume racing careers which had been so rudely interrupted in 1914; in most cases they were able to bring out their prewar machines and carry on from where they had left off. The new entrants to the industry had first to design and build the cars and motor-cycles which they hoped to race; this was a condition which greatly en-hanced the technical interest of Brook-lands racing during its second period. The vast expansion which had taken place in the design and production of aircraft and aero-engines had been accompanied by the wide dissemination of technological 'know-how' which previously had been confined to a small group; this resulted in a great stimulus to originality and invention, some of which would be applied to making cars go faster.

This last objective could also be attained by much simpler means. Among government surplus stocks

Above: Looking back from the end of the Member's Banking, the photographer records the first JCC 200 mile race. Below: Douglas Hawkes Morgan with special Anzani engine, overhead camshaft, in the 1922 200 miles race

were to be found numbers of high-powered aero-engines which could be purchased at a fraction of their original cost; from this source would arise a second generation of monster cars not so much designed as improvised by men whose enthusiasm was not always matched by their engineering competence or earlier experience. At the other end of the scale, there was soon to burst forth another revival eminently more practical and far-reaching in its consequences – the cycle-car, an attempt to combine the amenities of the motor-car with the early economy of the motor-cycle. It is not without justification that some have called this second Brooklands period a glorious 'free for all'.

Among the more notable new cars to appear on the track during the first postwar season were two designs by the redoubtable Coatalen; the first of them a 6-cylinder of five litres capacity and originally built for the 1919 Indianapolis 500 mile race, though

prevented from taking part. The other was a 'modern' monster driven by an 18-litre 12-cylinder Vee Sunbeam aero-engine. Three hundred horse-power in a car whose all-in weight was less than one and a half tons would obviously be capable of a fantastic performance, provided its driver could hold it on the track. It proved to be a car which made the heaviest demands upon the most accomplished drivers and for this reason added much to the spectacular attraction of Brooklands. It is open to question how far this car, or any of the other aero-engined monsters to follow, was effective in the improvement of the breed.

This same season saw the first appearance of a 'cycle-car' designed primarily with an eye to its perfor-

Chitty Chitty Bang Bang

mance on the race track. The basic idea of the cycle-car had occurred to a number of people during the early days without much practical result; it sprang into sudden popularity during 1912 with such effect that, before the year was out, there was formed the Cyclecar Club to cater exclusively for the new class of vehicle. Although none of its promoters could possibly be aware of the fact, the formation of this club was later to produce a profound influence upon the development of Brooklands. However, before this could transpire the club would change its name to Junior Car Club in response to the inevitable evolution of the cycle-car into the light motor-car; and Brooklands racing was a primary cause of that evolution.

From the point of view of its design the general concept of the new type of vehicle was a motor-cycle with two extra wheels for stability and a modicum of bodywork to provide some weather protection for the occupants. Looked at another way, it could be seen as a motor-car in which each functional structure and mechanism was reduced to the simplest form. The engine was a standard single or twin cylinder air-cooled type exactly as manufactured for motor-cycles: transmission was by vee belt or chain, duplicated to provide alternative gear-ratios, no reverse-gear being provided; the vehicles were so light as to be easily lifted at one end and turned round to face the other way: steering and braking were effected through systems comprising bobbins, pulleys, levers and stranded wire-cable. Track width between wheels was in some cases reduced to an absolute minimum by seating driver and passenger in tandem within a body no more than twenty-four inches wide. Among other extreme expedients, some of the makers dispensed with Ackermann steering and pivoted a rigid front-axle at its centre. It is astonishing to recall that in 1913 there were listed so many independent manufacturers, each manufacturing to his own designs.

These unconventional vehicles competed successfully among themselves in speed trials and hill climbs; a road race in France was won at a speed of more than 40mph. It should be noted, however, that the winner was a Morgan three-wheeler; a British machine which was later to achieve

Chitty Chitty Bang Bang in trouble after its crash in 1922

quite sensational success at Brooklands. As for the rest of the types, scarcely any of them were to be seen after the war; the outstanding exception was the GN, named after Godfrey and Frazer-Nash its originators and makers; from the beginning, this firm had avoided bizarre departures from conventional practice. Moreover, both men were engineers of no mean ability. During 1920, an improved GN won a Brooklands race at nearly 60mph; a year later, after further development it was breaking records at over 80mph. The cycle-car idea was dead; the light-car which replaced it would eventually develop into the prototype of the modern European motor-car and that development could not have taken place without Brooklands. The fundamental basis of light-car development was the progressive increase in the power obtained from unit cylinder capacity and that was the main business of Brooklands during the first and second periods of its existence; the process continued into the third period, but at a diminishing rate.

The year of 1921 was a veritable milestone in the history of Brooklands racing. It was marked by the infiltration (if that is an acceptable word) of an organising body separate from the BARC. It began when the Junior Car Club (successor to the Cycle Car Club) was allowed by the resident body to organise its own 200 mile race in the October of that year. This proved to be one of the most notable races ever to be run at Brooklands. The distance alone was enough to eliminate the last vestige of the horse racing tradition; being the first race to be staged by the JCC, it was possible for the organisers to lay their plans unhindered by precedent. In the event, the organisation was excellent. The race was run in two classes simultaneously, one limited to 1,500cc and the other to 1,100cc. Nearly forty cars came to the starting line, representing between them more than twenty different makes of vehicle; ten pairs, three trios, one foursome, a team of five, and the remainder individual. It was this grouping which added so much to the technical interest of the race.

The winning of a place by a single representative of a make of car is always creditable enough, but it does not necessarily provide conclusive

Many cars were entered for events at Brooklands and never reached the starting line. The Vegova 750cc (right) hopefully was entered for the 1924 200 mile race whilst the Light Humber 'Ikan Opitt' (above) and the rare 10hp Silver Hawk of T E Ellis (below) were both doubtful contestants

Above : Sir Malcolm Campbell in one of his Talbots , 24th September 1921
Below : A 1910 10-litre Fiat driven by Captain John Duff in the 1920 season

**Above : One of a few Horstman cars entered for the 1921 season
Below : T B Andre and his Marlborough at the Easter Meeting of 1921**

Alvis of Green and Dykes in a 3 litre
production race at Brooklands

Above : A typical Brooklands innovation of the 'free for all' period.
This Scriver- Special is an adaptation of a standard Austin twenty
Below : 'Silver Ghost' entered by A D Sanderson in the 1920 season.
Rolls-Royce feelings are not recorded

evidence of its quality ; in some respects the win might even have been a fluke. On the other hand, when a team of three cars secures the first three places with only a matter of seconds between each, there can be no doubt about the quality of the cars. Actually, it was only between first and second that the margin was so small owing to the fact that the third had suffered a burst tyre and thereby lost nearly four minutes ; until that happened, the three cars had run with clockwork regularity at a constant distance apart. The race was won at almost 90mph. The 1,100cc class was won by a GN at nearly 72mph.

The winning 1½-litre Talbot-Darracq's had been designed by Louis Coatalen, the firm of Sunbeam having become associated with the Talbot and Darracq concerns. The principal features of the engines closely resembled those of the Peugeot which Coatalen is alleged to have copied when designing the 1914 Grand Prix Sunbeam cars ; with four valves per cylinder and operated by twin overhead camshafts. Several of the other engines competing were of

Captain 'Archie' Frazer-Nash in a GN conversion at the 1920 season

nearly as advanced design ; the remainder being of more conventional type. Of course, it is one thing for an engine to embody advanced features in terms of its verbal specification ; it is entirely another to realise their potential through the appropriate quality of detail design ; inadequate design applied to an advanced specification will prove much inferior to some 'old-fashioned' specification designed by a master. The principle was amply demonstrated in course of the race.

It has already been remarked how much easier it is to design and build an engine that shall be capable of winning short races as against one capable of maintaining its performance over 200 miles. Quite a number of the cars started off in fine style only to peter out, one by one, as various mechanical weaknesses revealed themselves. In some cases it could have been simply a matter of wear and tear ; few earlier races had been preceeded by so much

Above : Start of a JCC High Speed Trial for standard cars. Left : Parry Thomas superintends refinements to his ill-fated 'Babs'. Below : A 1913 200hp Benz still going strong in the nineteen-twenties. The Birkin blown Bentley can be seen beyond

practising beforehand. A very noticeable feature was the near absence of tyre failure, due largely, no doubt, to the light weight of the competing cars; progress in tyre construction was to be more reliably assessed by the performance of the aero-engined monsters.

There were two factors which made this first 200 mile race so important. It brought together a representative assembly of cars many of whose designers had sought to incorporate the whole body of experience which had been accumulated since the time when Brooklands was first opened. It is not suggested that all this experience had been gained exclusively on the track, though a good deal of it had been so gained; no other place offered the same opportunities. It must be admitted that most of this progress had been directed towards a somewhat circumscribed end – the steady increase of power-output from unit cylinder capacity. The race had provided the further opportunity of ascertaining how far this increase of efficiency had been gained without loss of reliability. Great progress had been made, but there still remained a long way to go.

A similar pattern of development was discernable among the racing motorcycles, though progress here was at a much slower rate. There were a number of reasons to account for this. The war had effectively removed the state of ignorance and prejudice which had so long impeded acceptance of the motor-car; its unlimited scope as a utility vehicle for purposes of business and recreation was now fully recognised. It was clearly seen that the only factor limiting sales was cost. There were two ways of tackling this problem although only one of them was visible (or even possible) at the time – reduction in the size of engine which, in turn, would permit reduction in size and weight of the complete car. The alternative approach through production in vast quantities had yet to be developed. Henry Ford was blazing the trail in America and had already established a factory in England, but the famous Model T lacked one characteristic essential to the European market: snob appeal.

General utility was something which could never be claimed for the motorcycle; from the beginning, its essential appeal was to the sporting instincts of the younger generation, a class inevitably short of ready cash. Older men might have the money, but they were not attracted by a form of transport which required the wearing of heavy and unsightly outer garments plus the final disfigurement of a pair of goggles. With all this equipment it was still not possible to keep clean; the necessity of disrobing and having a good wash before keeping an appointment was a fatal drawback. Over and above these objections was the ever-present risk of sideslip on muddy roads pockmarked with horse droppings.

Prestige through ownership of a motor-car was closely associated with that peculiar dignity deriving from the combination of power with silence. Dignity was for ever denied the motorcyclist and he was more likely to seek prestige through the ear-splitting note of his engine's open exhaust. Then there was the question of speed. The fastest cars in the 1921 JCC 200 mile race could lap Brooklands at little short of 100mph, whereas the average 1½-litre car then on sale to the public might not be capable of attaining a mile a minute and was more likely to be driven by its owner at around 40mph. Against this, practically any contemporary 500cc motor-cycle could be taken straight from the showroom and ridden at well over 60mph. If the purchaser wished to travel really fast, he could buy a standard 1,000cc twin and straightway exceed eighty; although few such purchasers would have possessed the aptitude or the foolhardiness to make the attempt.

Unlike the case of the motor-car, motor-cycle manufacturers had little

A good attendance on Members' Hill

FRED CAPEL
EST 20 YEARS

incentive to design and build engines of much smaller cylinder capacity which would develop the same power as the current models. Reference has already been made to the fact that the general proportions of a stable motor-cycle are more or less independent of engine capacity. Motor-cycle manufacturers were no less aware of the advertisement to be obtained from success in racing; they were fortunate in the circumstances which enabled them to get the advertisement without spending large sums of money; money which few of them could spare in any case. There were numbers of amateur (and quasi-amateur) riders who had learned the art of tuning engines through their war-time service with aircraft. These men proceeded to obtain from engines performances which sometimes surprised their manufacturers. In addition, there appeared a few new makes of machine designed and manufactured by young engineers who had learned their craft in the design offices of the aero-engine firms.

During and since the war, a great deal of research into the operation of the internal combustion engine had been carried out by Harry Ricardo, research which revolutionised the performance of side-valve engines in particular and established the octane rating of fuels. For reasons which remain a matter for conjecture, the influence of Ricardo's work became apparent in motor-cycle racing long before it affected the racing-car; a number of people designed their own cylinder-heads in accordance with Ricardo's teachings and fitted them to otherwise standard engines. A notable exception of this tardiness on the part of the car industry was the commissioning of Ricardo by Vauxhall to design in their entirety the engines for their new Grand Prix cars. However, it takes much longer to design and build new cars than it does to provide a new cylinder-head.

It was this kind of freelance activity which justifies description of Brooklands' second period as a 'free for all'. Motor-cycle race meetings never drew the big crowds; instead they consistently attracted the same few hundreds of devoted enthusiasts, for the most part highly informed on technical matters; between competitors and spectators there existed a peculiar affinity which was never even approached in the sphere of car racing. Incidentally, it was not unusual to find leading racing drivers among the spectators at these meetings. It might at first seem surprising to find that motor-cycle race meetings enjoyed much greater freedom from accident, fatalities being nearly unknown. This may be explained by the inherent instability of a motor-cycle giving its rider immediate warning of any abnormality; moreover, every part of his machine was continuously visible to him. If by chance he should be thrown off, he would most likely roll along the ground in his leather clothing clear of his machine; provided he collided with no obstruction, he would usually be little the worse for the experience. On the other hand, all sorts of mechanical emergencies could happen in a racing car unbeknown to the driver until too late to respond. If the car crashed, the driver would most probably still be inside it; if he should get thrown out, there was a chance that the car might overtake him.

With the resumption of motor-cycle racing after the war, speeds tended to increase although only slowly and with a marked difference between the smallest and largest engine capacities. Speeds of the big 1,000cc twins changed hardly at all, while those of the smallest began to rise perceptibly. Profiting by Ricardo's researches, people began to experiment with much higher compression-ratios in small-bore cylinders. The next step was to run their engines on alcohol instead of petrol; with the result that some of the smallest engines were soon operating with compression-ratios of as high as nine to one as against the five to one of the big machines. By such means it became a much more rewarding business to attack records in the small classes rather than in the larger. So there began the same pursuit of higher power output from unit cylinder capacity as was happening with racing cars, but arising from quite a different motive.

It will be apparent that in both spheres these developments were of a highly technical nature, whether they were the work of large organisations or of independent freelances; not so the contemporary efforts being made to fit larger and larger engines into any likely chassis which might by lying around. This is not to question either the integrity or the technical competence of those concerned. They were, first and foremost, great sportsmen; the point to be made is that their cars – the 'modern' monsters – could not be said to have been designed: they were improvisations, a collection of adaptations put together. The first and by far the most famous was Count Zborowski's 'Chitty Bang Bang' which made its first public appearance at Brooklands in 1921.

Motor racing could be said to have run in the family, Zborowski's father having been unfortunately killed at a French hill climb in 1903. The Count was to suffer a similar fate in the 1924 Grand Prix at Monza; by a coincidence, both lost their lives when driving Mercedes cars. Chitty Bang Bang No 1 comprised a 23-litre Maybach aero-engine installed in a prewar Mercedes chain-drive chassis; this was obviously a monster with a vengeance. The Count's principal assistant in later stages of this enterprise was Clive Gallop with whom, in the middle thirties, I came to be closely associated in business; from him I learned something of difficulties which had to be overcome in this fantastic task of adaptation; he freely confessed how often judgement had to give way to expediency. From its first appearance on the track this car won immortal fame, far exceeding in popu-

View from top of the banking towards the Railway Straight – a London bound train is in the background

larity the 12-cylinder aero-engined Sunbeam which Coatalen had introduced the previous year. In addition to being a masterly driver, Zborowski was also something of a showman and the combination made a great appeal to the Brooklands crowd.

From now on there would be, so to speak, two faces to Brooklands racing – a continuing pursuit of greater power from unit cylinder capacity, enlivened by battles between the giants. Obviously, the drivers of these monsters could never become involved in the struggle for efficiency for the simple reason that their cars were already too fast for the track; their performance was limited not by their engines but by the skill and courage of their drivers. For a given output per litre, power will be obviously proportional to the cube-root of engine power, a car of Chitty Bang Bang's capacity would be capable of two and a half times the speed of the $1\frac{1}{2}$-litre Talbot-Darracq's; that is to say, nearly 250mph!

This first of Zborowksi's cars seemed, in his hands at any rate, to behave very well; the same could not be said of another aero-engined car soon to follow – the Wolseley Viper. Built under the direction of that same Alastair Miller who was earlier noticed on a Matchless motor-cycle performing peculiar gyrations on the Byfleet Banking in 1912, this car carried a 12-litre Hispano-

Suiza aero-engine in an old Napier chassis. Curiously enough, the car appeared to suffer an inherent tendency to imitate the Matchless when negotiating the banking. As might be expected, all these aero-engined cars were difficult to handle for the simple reason that they were improvisations. There still continued to race one or two of the prewar monsters and it was interesting to observe their relative behaviour.

It need hardly be said that the collective performances of all these big-engined cars provided the high-spot at BARC race meetings; lap speeds in the neighbourhood of 120mph began to be taken for granted. However, they were by no means the only source of interest. Distributed between all the other classes, there raced a host of different makes, any one of which was worthy of report; if the speeds of the monsters were taken for granted, there was never-failing interest in observing how the performances of all the other cars were climbing up. One way and another, this middle period of Brooklands racing was fascinating to a degree. This fascination was not exclusively confined to the circuit. Happy hours could be spent in the Paddock where, to the accompanying sound of idling engines, suggestive of the roll of distant gunfire, and amidst the aroma of Castrol oil, detailed examination

could be made of any new arrival to the track. The drivers were often just as interesting as the vehicles they drove; there was no means of telling whether any one of them would quickly blossom as a Brooklands star or just fade away into oblivion.

At about this time there appeared a driver who was to make history; his début was all the more impressive on account of the complete absence of fuss and noise surrounding it. The story had been told before how a gifted and experienced chief-engineer, who had first learned to drive not so very long before, brought his latest luxury model in order to demonstrate its gentlemanly behaviour and stayed to become per-

haps the best known of Brooklands drivers. Parry Thomas proceeded to lap at a speed of more than 100mph in a standard Leyland straight-eight of 7-litre capacity. The silent grace with which the car performed was a revelation. Thomas went on to design a number of special racing cars which were uniformly successful; every one of them was a demonstration of what could be achieved when a first class engineer had the freedom to design a racing car from scratch. As time passed, it became evident that love of driving was taking precedence over his interest in design; he had already broken the lap record at almost 130-mph and the half mile at 137mph when he decided to acquire the late Zborowski's last creation, the 'Higham Special' – later re-named 'Babs' by Thomas. It was a fateful purchase.

The Higham Special was the result of a joint effort by Zborowski and Gallop, centred round a 27-litre Liberty aero-engine. After a few sensational appearances at Brooklands, Thomas took it to Pendine Sands in South Wales and raised the world speed record to the neighbourhood of 170mph. Going out later to improve upon this figure, a rear-chain apparently broke and be-headed the driver. It was a tragic accident. I had met Thomas not very long before; he was associated with the Brooklands engineering firm of Thomson and Taylor which had done a vast amount of work on various Brooklands cars. Plans were under discussion for the modification, manufacture and marketing of Thomas's straight-eight engines. This preparatory work necessitated the closest examination and study of the drawings, accompanied by a running discourse on the part of their designer. I was immensely impressed by Thomas's engineering philosophy; it seemed a shocking waste of talent that such a man should be hazarding his life testing tyres to destruction at Brooklands.

CHANGE OF COURSE

Brooklands racing became progressively more interesting as its second period advanced; chiefly on account of ever-increasing variety of both cars and drivers. Much of the interest before the war had centred around the sustained rivalry between the firms of Sunbeam and Vauxhall. This competition continued in a different form; it was now between cars rather than people. Coatalen was as active as ever producing new designs which his company manufactured; direct participation by Vauxhall became less discernible after Pomeroy had left for America. A few of their cars continued to be raced by private owners while the company concentrated its efforts towards quantity production of its standard models. There was no lack of new arrivals to fill the gap. It was in the 1,500 and 1,100cc classes that competition became most acute; with their first 200 mile race the Junior Car Club had started more than they had realised. Manufacturers of light cars turned their attention to special racing cars, while most of the leading drivers sought membership of the JCC so that they might be eligible to drive them in the next 'two-hundred'.

So great had been the impetus of the prewar cycle-car movement that more than seventy different makes of light-car were exhibited at the 1922 motor show in London. Not all of these makes were to be seen at Brooklands and by no means all the cars which did race had been specially designed for that purpose. The 'Sports Car', was coming into vogue, the equivalent of the 'TT' motor-cycle which had long been on the market; these were production models modified to give higher performance. The cars which ran in the successive 200 mile races included both categories. Some idea of the intensity of technical effort inspired by those races will be apparent from the table below.

	1921	1922
1st	Talbot Darracq	Talbot Darracq
2nd	Talbot Darracq	Aston Martin
3rd	Talbot Darracq	Talbot Darracq
	89mph	88mph

	1923	1924
1st	Alvis	Talbot Darracq
2nd	Bugatti	Talbot Darracq
3rd	AC	Talbot Darracq
	93mph	102mph

The astonishing consistency of the Talbot Darracq's is too obvious to require comment, bearing in mind that the team did not run in 1923. What is worthy of mention is the tremendous effort which must have been made by the Aston Martin concern to break the Talbot Darracq sequence and by the Alvis company to raise the winning speed by five miles per hour. It is not surprising that Talbot Darracq deemed it advisable to resort to supercharging before returning to the fray in 1924. Another outstanding feature of this last race was the winning of the smaller class by a 750cc Austin Seven at 76mph. Thus may be seen the very great advance in engine performance during the first five years after reopening of the track.

Up to this time, the whole emphasis had been on engine development, for

Extemporized road-racing on a Brooklands service-road

the simple reason that normal Brooklands racing did not make any special demands on the car as a whole, provided that the chassis was of reasonable design and construction. In fact, some of the normal functions such as alternative gear-ratios and even brakes were sometimes dispensed with in order to obtain a little more speed. Earlier, there had been the classic occasion when all the oil was drained from a Vauxhall back-axle in order to obtain a marginal increase of speed required to break a record. However, it was not with a view to technical development that, in 1925, the Junior Car Club introduced the first of a series of obstructions and diversions such as would render gear-changes and braking a vital factor in the winning of races. The essential purpose of these innovations was to introduce an element of the spectacular as a means of drawing larger numbers of spectators.

SALMSON

The famous Talbot–Darracq team which had such success in 1921, 1922 and 1924

14
12

It has always been the giant cars travelling at well over 100mph which had so far provided such spectacle as might be found. The interest of spectators in the smaller cars had been largely technical and associated with the progressive increase of speed. Now that 1½-litre cars could travel at more than the 'hundred' their special claim to interest had largely disappeared; they could be seen as poor imitators of their larger brothers. The first of these diversions from the main (outer) circuit was brought into operation at the 200 mile race of 1925 and took the simple form of using half the length of the Finishing Straight as a two-way loop. As cars came off the Byfleet Banking they came into this straight, made a U-turn round a barrier and travelled in the reverse direction and turned left at the Fork; here they resumed their broken journey towards the Members' Banking. By these means the spectators were titillated by the thrills of watching at close quarters the cornering skill of the drivers.

The following year there was introduced for the 200 mile race a variation of the plan. Cars now continued the full length of the Finishing Straight, negotiating on the way a fairly sharp S-bend formed by means of sandbags; after passing through this bend they continued towards the outer circuit and rejoined it by a left turn just before the Railway Straight. With this arrangement, the section containing the Members' Banking was by-passed. Both of these arrangements reduced lap speeds by more·than 20mph, but this was considered of no importance against the additional interest of the cornering.

A further variation was obtained by turning right at the end of the Finishing Straight and travelling round the Members' Banking in the reverse direction; then proceeding as far as the Fork and, by means of a right-hand turn, back into the Finishing Straight.

Waiting to line up for the start of the 1930 'Double Twelve'

**Above : Bookmakers were usually found near the lap-scoring-board
Left : But bets could also be placed in the Paddock . Below : F B Halford's
1½ litre special preparing for a start**

This complete encircling of the Members' Hill was known as the Mountain Circuit. It was not until 1938 that a new length of track was added to the course. This addition was not 100 feet wide, but represented an ordinary roadway comprising two sections. The first of these ran from a point along the Railway Straight, across the area contained within the main circuit, to a point near the Fork; along its course occurred a hairpin bend and an 'easy' lefthand right-angle bend. Opposite, on the other side of the Finishing Straight, the second section ran for some distance parallel with that Straight and almost adjacent to it; at a point in line with the Paddock, a sharp hairpin bend led to a short section which joined the outer circuit at the beginning of the Members' Banking. These new roads, used in conjunction with that part of the outer circuit including the Members' Banking, were known as the Campbell Circuit; so named after Sir Malcolm Campbell whose idea it was. It thus became possible to provide at Brooklands a fair simulation of road racing conditions where the whole motor-car could be tested with the same severity as had been applied to engines. The Campbell Circuit came too late to achieve very much; it is a pity nobody had thought of it before.

The intense interest of the second period of Brooklands racing derived not only from the machines, but equally from the men who raced them. There was one important difference between the two. The machines either became worn out or their performance became obsolete; their drivers and riders, through sheer practice and cumulative experience, gradually became masters of their art – or at least some of them did. Just as it is impossible here to mention even a small percentage of the machines which were raced on the track, so it is with the drivers; names are mentioned only so far as they illustrate the general theme. When making a survey of the whole life of Brooklands, it remains for ever astonishing that the vast majority of drivers and riders survived the perils of racing and, when the time came, moved on to other fields of activity. The fact that serious accidents were so few is a testimony to the design, organisation and maintenance of the track; far more is it testimony to the quality of the men who rode and drove.

It is impossible to mention any of them without giving first place to that doyen of Brooklands, Sir Malcolm Campbell. His first reported appearance was in 1911 when he drove a Darracq. The following year, I made his acquaintance as the rider of a Triumph motor-cycle in between his performances on the Darracq. Twenty-five years later, he was still driving in Brooklands races; altogether he must have driven more different cars than any other man. He experienced many narrow escapes, including the finishing of a race after both the near side wheels of his car had collapsed. He was a most likeable person and the friend of everybody who raced at Brooklands. When away for any length of time from the track, he was usually breaking world speed records elsewhere, such as when he became the first man to drive a car at 300mph or exceeding a speed of 140mph on water. Truly, a most remarkable career. It was fitting that when, in 1936, the ownership of the track was changed, Sir Malcolm became one of the directors of the new company.

A few other latter-day drivers began their track careers before the First World War, although the great majority made their first appearance during the second period of Brooklands racing. One who, within a shorter time, drove nearly as great a variety of racing-cars as Campbell was Kaye Don who went on to become one of the masters consistently capable of lapping the track at around 140mph. He attracted notice in 1921 by breaking records in an AC 1¾-litre car, travelling nearly 95 miles in the hour. At that time, Don would ride or drive anything which was likely to add to his experience. He was then Sales-Manager

Above: Americans were a rare sight at Brooklands – Stutz arrives for the 1929 'Double Twelve'. **Below:** One of the 'Dutch Clog' Austin Sevens adapted for record-breaking

The first stage of the track seen from the air above point 1

Junction of the Finishing Straight with Members' Banking seen from point 2

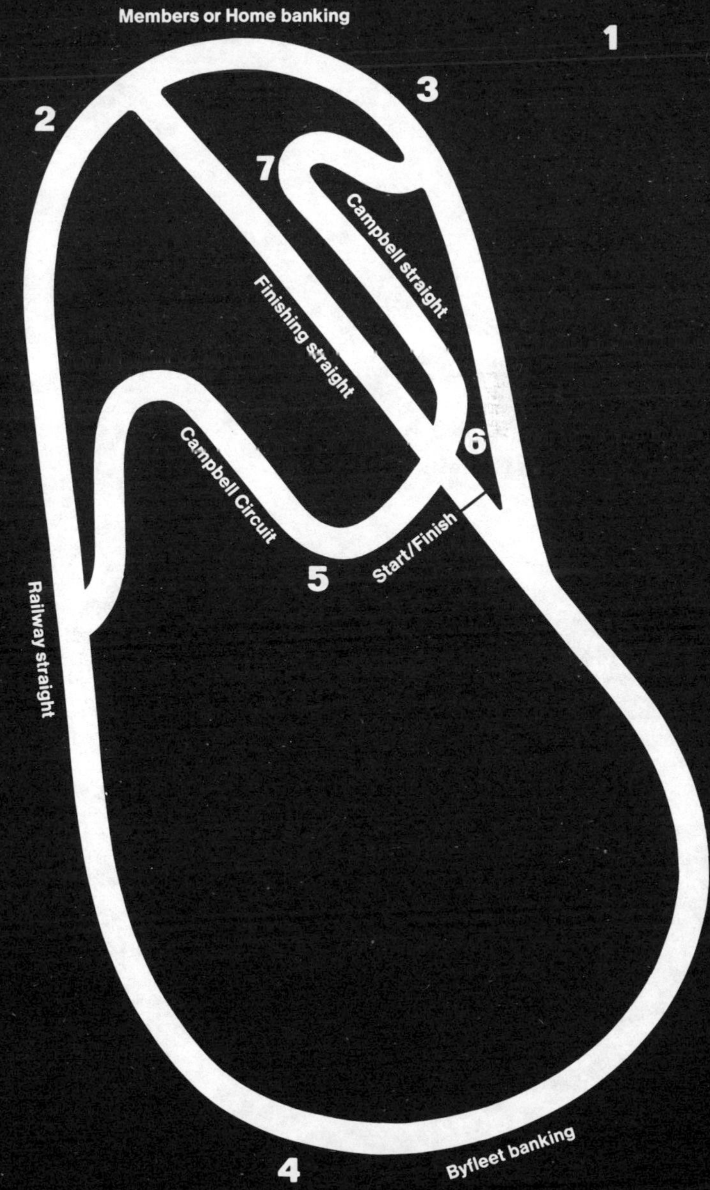

Brooklands motor race circuit

The Club-Members' Enclosure and Members' Banking seen from point 3

The beginning of the Byfleet seen from point 4

'Central' section of the Campbell Circuit from point 5

The beginning of the Members' Banking as seen from point 6

The Finishing Straight from point 7 before the building of the Campbell Circuit

to the Avon Tyre Company and it was in that capacity that I first met him. Mentioning that I owned a special racing motor-cycle which was very tricky to handle, especially as I had recently been involved in a road-accident, Don immediately offered to ride it at Brooklands without fee or reward. He mastered the machine, but failed to get a place, for even in those days his reputation was sufficient to allot him a handicap which could not be overcome in a short race. Kaye Don was a great driver and a very hand-some one into the bargain. Towards the end, he was a star of the track, con-sistently lapping at the highest speeds without, so far as I am aware, ever being involved in an accident.

As the second period of Brooklands racing passed imperceptibly into the third, it was unavoidable that the pro-fessional element should begin to

Richard Marker's Bentley–Jackson special overtakes an MG Magnette

Lagonda in the 1929 6 hour Endurance Test

predominate, if only by virtue of in-creasing speeds. In the early days when, for the greater part, speeds were much lower and races could be won at sixty or seventy miles an hour, almost any amateur with a good machine and the knowledge necessary to tune it stood a very good chance of an occasional win. At 80 and 90mph things began to become more difficult and only a few could hold a car at much more than the 'hundred'. Moreover, there were very few stock cars at that time which were capable of such speeds; even if they were, their track-worthiness might be very ques-tionable. Then, quite apart from driving ability, the steady growth of mechnical complexity tended to put any amateur, except for the more wealthy, out of the racing business. A milestone along this path of increasing complexity and cost was marked by the introduction of supercharging.

The principle of supercharging de-pends upon the driving by the engine of a compressor which is capable of forcing into the engine cylinders a greater mass of air than can otherwise be inhaled. Power is consumed in driving the compressor, although not as much as can be gained by its proper use. It is necessary on practical grounds that a supercharger should be driven at a rotational speed several times that of the engine. It follows that these high speeds of rotation introduce many mechnical problems so that, one way and another, a supercharged engine is not suited to amateur use. The advent of supercharging also introduced a new set of problems to the organisers of races. Strictly speaking, a 1½-litre engine when supercharged ceases to be a 1½ litre engine if, as would pro-perly be the case, the capacity of an engine is to be calculated according to the volume of air actually inhaled into the engine from the atmosphere when operating at a volumetric efficiency of 100 per cent. Apart from use with the two-stroke cycle, the rational field for the supercharger is confined to piston type aero-engines and certain types of marine engine; with the gas-turbine engine, supercharging in the normal sense of the word loses its meaning. For purposes of motor racing it has become the general practice to rate supercharged and unsupercharged engines separately. Upon their introduction to Brooklands, superchargers were not held to change the capacity-rating of a car.

With these technical details out of the way, a more effective comparison can be made between respective prospects of an aspiring amateur in 1909 and another in the middle '30s or even earlier. In 1909, W O Bentley (who later was to design successful aero-engines and, later still, Bentley cars), rode a 5hp Rex motor-cycle at Brooklands; if he bought the simply constructed machine new, it probably cost him about fifty pounds; it is doubtful if it could do much over 60mph. By way of contrast let us consider the situation, twenty or more years later, of an amateur well informed on the early days of Brooklands and feeling a strong urge to obtain first-hand experience.

On grounds of economy, he might first consider motor-cycle racing and decide to visit the track in the first instance as spectator. After watching motor-cycles lapping at 100mph he might well have second thoughts and conclude that four wheels would be better than two, even though it would mean spending more money. In forming an idea of what would be required he might well base his estimate on the current activity of another designer of aero-engines (both past and future) namely F B Halford. He would have found this driver also travelling at over the 'hundred' in his supercharged 6-cylinder $1\frac{1}{2}$-litre Halford-Special and come to the conclusion that the cost would be prohibitive. It would equally be clear that he had neither the skill nor the time to undertake the maintenance and tuning of so complex a mechanism;

thus there would be added to a exorbitant investment the heavy cost of specialist services. Neither could he be certain that he could handle the car if he bought one; it was one thing to have started when speeds were low and gradually acquire expertise as they increased; it was quite another to 'plunge in at the deep-end'.

The full extent of the changes which the passage of years had wrought become starkly apparent when we find that our imaginary amateur would have found that by far the cheapest (and probably the safest) way in which to share the pleasures of Brooklands was to take to the air in an aeroplane. Unlike A V Roe, there would have been no necessity to undertake the building of his own machine or to buy one from somebody else and teach himself to fly. At a modest outlay he could have joined the Brooklands Flying Club and then, whenever he felt so disposed, make a telephone call to arrange an hour's flying instruction for forty shillings. With the benefits of expert instruction and perfectly reliable engines, there would be no need to worry about immersion in the sewage farm for that risk had become a thing of the past. It is true that he would have been denied the unique pleasure of the Blue Bird Restaurant because, unfortunately, this was burned to the ground during its wartime occupation.

The view has often been expressed that the exhibition of looping-the-loop and other aerobatics by Pégoud in 1913 marked a turning-point in flying at Brooklands; it disposed of certain inhibitions and gave to pilots a new sense of freedom which they were not slow to develop. During that year there were trained many pupils who in later life would attain great distinction, not least Lord Dowding who commanded Fighter Command during the Battle of Britain. In an unbelievably short period of time, some of the hangars began to be taken over for aeroplane manufacture on a small scale; of these, the firm of Vickers was to remain longest and eventually buy the whole Brook-

Climbing the Test Hill in the early 1930s

lands establishment. Their Vimy Bomber which was to be the first aeroplane to fly the Atlantic non-stop was tested there as was the first Hawker Hurricane fighter. The full 'Roll of Honour' of Brooklands is almost without end.

The time was to come, after motor racing and flying-club had ceased, when the phrase 'Roll of Honour' would acquire a more sombre hue. During the First World War, the firm of Vicker's had built extensive workshops immediately outside the track at the Fork; so close indeed that the doors comprised the boundary of the concrete. At the outbreak of the Second World War these premises had been greatly extended while, within the aerodrome, another works had been erected for the assembly of Hawker aeroplanes. As a centre for manufacture and repair of aircraft, Brook-

lands had assumed considerable military importance and thus, in common with all other aircraft establishments, an obvious target for German bombs. A heavy air-raid in 1940 resulted in heavy damage and more than 600 casualties. These manufacturing facilities were subsequently dispersed to less vulnerable sites; among those who remained behind were Barnes Wallis and his personal staff, now housed in the BARC club house in the Paddock. Here, where in 1911 a shilling-tea had been so much enjoyed, there was now to be evolved the 'dam-buster' bomb and those other inventions of Barnes Wallis which contributed so much to ultimate victory for the Allies.

THE DAWN OF PROFESSIONALISM

The first and second periods of Brooklands racing were separated by five years of military occupation of the track; it is not so easy to define exactly where the second period ended and the third began, for the one merged imperceptibly into the other. The third period is to be identified by decline of the 'free-for-all' and a marked increase in the 'professional' element. The word 'professionalism' applies to two aspects of what is much the same thing – the pursuit of financial reward as a main objective, and the intensive cultivation of exceptional skill necessary to success in that pursuit. We are here concerned with only the second aspect. Whether or not a driver were interested in financial reward, the cost of racing progressively increased (in· terms of both money and time) as racing became more sophisticated. In the previous chapter, the transition has been related to the advent of supercharging and the introduction of artificial corners.

The difficulties and dangers of cornering are measured by the centri-fugal force generated in making the turn. The force is proportional to the square of the speed of the car and inversely proportional to the radius of curvature; if the centrifugal force is great enough, it will cause the car to skid or overturn. Now it will be evident that in travelling round the outer circuit of Brooklands, cornering was involved just as much as when negotiating the artificial hazards. The difference between the two cases being that when negotiating the banking there was only one variable, namely the speed of the car in relation to its position on the banking; only by exceeding a known limit was the driver in danger of going over the top. Once a driver had acquired adequate familiarity with the outer circuit, the need for practice was limited to tuning his car to go faster and, if required, this could be done on suitable roads away from the track. The only cost was in petrol, oil, tyres and wear and tear of engine.

Circumstances attaching to practice for the artificial corners were entirely

Making a start on the Finishing Straight for the 1934 International Trophy

different. To begin with, there were two fundamental variables instead of one – the radius of curvature of the path chosen by the driver as well as the speed at which he chose to take that path. The opportunities of practicing on the actual circuit were restricted to the limited time the obstacles might be in position, whereas the learning of the art of cornering is inherently a very protracted business. Consequently, the bulk of practice must be done elsewhere; the many and serious objections to this arrangement will be obvious. The really vital factor is that the essential purpose of all this practice will be to learn just how far the driver might go without actually overturning the car. Clearly, any serious attempt to master the art of cornering must of necessity involve risks of damage and personal injury which cannot be calculated in advance; a condition which many amateurs simply could not afford.

The later years of Brooklands were marked by increasingly strict surveillance of intending competitors; this was a necessary and very proper precaution on the part of authority. A mediocre driver taking too high a path on the banking in relation to his speed could not only obstruct faster drivers but also imperil their safety. Similarly on the road circuits; a driver going too slowly or taking too wide a sweep round an obstacle could be a menace to more skilful and faster drivers. So, in the present context, the term 'professional' is intended to cover those riders and drivers who, by virtue of their phenomenal skill (sometimes amounting to genius) were able consistently to ride and drive at speeds far beyond those which, on any rational basis, could be considered 'safe'.

If questions should be asked as to the criteria by which any speed might be adjudged 'safe', it would be difficult to give a satisfactory answer;

Above : Briefing the drivers before a race. Percy Bradley (last Clerk of Course) reads the rules. Below : View of the Campbell Circuit

Above : Kay Don in happy mood. Below : John Cobb seated in the Napier-Railton ; the combination which set the all-time lap record of 143.4mph

there were too many factors to take into consideration – the car, the driver, the state of the track, the weather and many things besides. Then there was the question of time, in more senses than one. What was safe for a couple of laps might not be safe for fifty. What was safe in 1939 might have been highly dangerous in 1909 and *vice-versa*. Neither could accidents provide a reliable guide.; there were not enough of them to provide a statistical basis; moreover, the causes were too varied and sometimes unknown. An isolated accident due to mechnical failure might prove nothing; in any case, the discovery of hidden mechanical weakness was among the original purposes of Brooklands.

The truth of the matter, surely, is that motor racing always was, and remains, a highly dangerous and therefore irrational activity, and one cannot reason about the irrational. Even the opinion that sheer speed must be a vital factor was contradicted in the only fatal accident at Brooklands of which I happened to be an immediate witness. A spectator, riding towards the Paddock at about 35mph after the close of a BMCRC race meeting, was thrown over the handle bars as the result of a broken driving belt jamming the back-wheel. He landed on the top of his head and broke his neck.

There was one hazard, much discussed already, which remained throughout the life of Brooklands, namely tyres; design and construction improved immensely, but the rate of advance was not fast enough. The amazing thing is that, although lap speeds increased towards 140mph, many drivers were able to hold their cars after a tyre had burst. One of the most remarkable things about Brooklands is that so many things changed in the course of the thirty-two years of its

Full circle. In April 1937, some thirty years after his famous 24-hour record run, S F Edge returned to Brooklands to open the new Campbell Circuit

152

The relaxing atmosphere continued even in the professional days

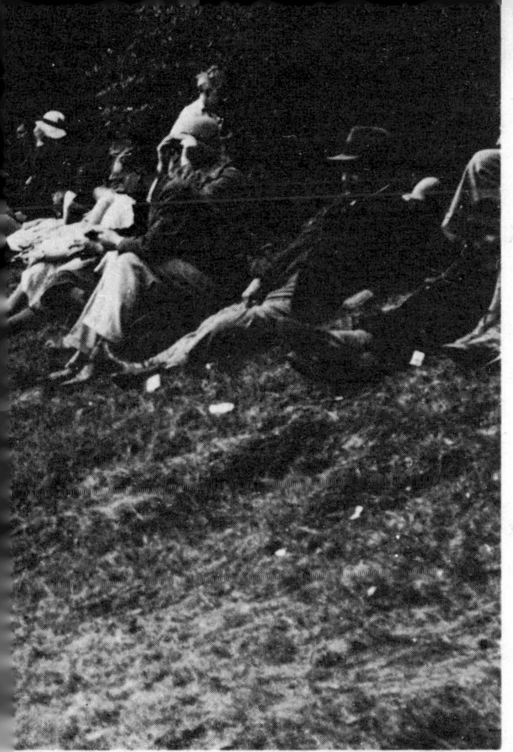

racing life yet so many other things remained the same. The division of that life into three periods was a subjective impression real enough to those who had known the track in its early days; it could scarcely be apparent to those who came later. It could therefore prove both interesting and informative to attempt some comparison between them.

Comparative maximum recorded speed irrespective of engine capacity is not particularly significant; the increase of little more than twenty miles per hour over the 128mph recorded in 1909 simply reveals the physical limitations imposed by the track. When Parry Thomas took his 'Babs' to Pendine Sands he was straightway able to exceed 170mph, a speed for which even the Members' Banking at Brooklands was totally inadequate; it was never designed for anything of the kind.

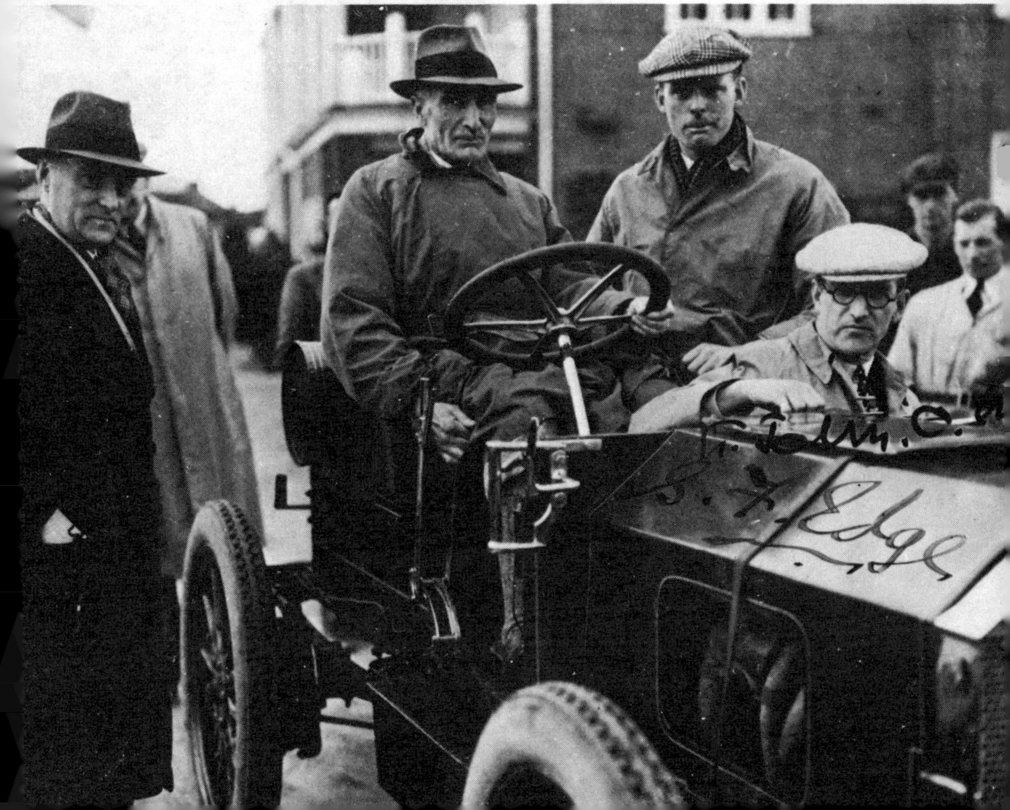

Thomas is believed to have exceeded 160mph with this car on the Railway Straight and then to have experienced difficulty in braking hard enough to slow sufficiently for entry onto the Byfleet Banking. Sustained speed over much longer distances is much more significant.

In 1907, during the famous twenty-four hour run by the Napier cars, S F Edge completed the first 200 miles at a speed of 69mph; the two accompanying cars were two or three miles per hour slower. In 1924, the JCC 200 mile race was won by a Talbot Darracq at 102.27 mph; second and third places were gained by two cars of similar make at 102.25 and 102.24mph respectively. In 1931, the British Racing Drivers Club 500 mile race was won at 118mph. Finally, in 1937, the BRDC 500 kilometre race was won by Cobb in the Napier-Railton car at 127mph. These figures alone will indicate the rising tide of professionalism which distinguished the later years of Brooklands. It may be seen still more clearly in the figures for the annual award of badges to those drivers achieving a lap speed of 120 mph. One was awarded in 1921; none in 1922, but one in each succeeding year up to and including 1927. Then the annual number began to increase sub-stantially until 1935 when twenty-one badges were awarded. Specially to be noted is the fact that the full list of 120 mph badge-holders included the names of five women drivers, two of whom further graduated to membership of that yet more distinguished band, totalling seventeen drivers in all, who achieved laps at 130mph or over.

No less distinguished were those who established records on both Mountain Circuit and Campbell Circuit where average speeds were necessarily much lower due to the many corners which had to be negotiated; success on these circuits demanded skill and expertise

One of the handful of cars to top 140mph at Brooklands was this Multi-Union driven by W C Devereaux in 1938

8

...ST FOR SPEED & COMFORT
F 643
44
F 89
FC 153
8

Raymond Mays' ERA in the 1937 JCC International Trophy race

of a very high order and, in addition, mastery of the outer-circuit, or parts of it at any rate. This 'new' kind of Brooklands racing certainly made a wider appeal to the public, attracting people who came solely for the sake of the spectacle. Similarly, with later racing on the outer circuit, people came to watch their favourite drivers rather than their favourite cars or make of car. Of course, there were many who continued to come for the same reasons as had prompted them to come in the earlier days; nevertheless, the general 'tone' of the Brooklands crowd had undergone a subtle change with the passing years.

Some old timers regretted the change and complained that the track had been turned into a circus, while others regarded it as a natural development which, in fact, it was. The original objective of Locke King and his associates had been twofold – to provide facilities whereby the motor-car

A touch of irony when the organisers staged this race for veteran cars. The occasion was the last race-meeting to be held at Brooklands – August 1939

industry could improve its products, and to finance this enterprise by entertainment of the general public. Both these objectives were attained; but after the motor-car had reached a certain stage of development Brooklands became increasingly redundant to further progress, whereas the need for entertainment of the public goes on for ever. Before 1939, there were on the market numbers of standard models capable of being driven in comfort and safety by private owners over long distances with complete reliability and at the fastest speeds which road conditions permitted. No longer did manufacturers depend upon advertisement of competition successes for their sales; the dominating factor had become selling price, acceptable performance was taken for granted.

The fact that the technical objective had been attained was no reason why the second objective, entertainment, should cease; it was only logical that the spectacular element of racing should be carried to the limit. Whether Brooklands could have held its own indefinitely against the more sophisticated circuits which have since come into existence is a very open question. It is a question which can never be answered. At the outbreak of the Second World War, the track was requisitioned as it had been in 1914 and given over entirely to purposes of military aviation and aircraft manufacture. The circumstances under which, at the end of the war, the owners of Brooklands decided to sell the whole property to the firm of Vickers Ltd have never been entirely clear; let it suffice that the decision caused widespread regret because it was seen to eliminate all hope of resuming motor racing.

It is hoped that in the course of these pages there will have emerged some recognisable picture of that phase in the development of the motor-car the passing of which continues to evoke so deep a measure of nostalgic regret; it is all contained in that single word Brooklands.

BROOKLANDS
AUTOMOBILE
RACING
CLUB
OFFICIAL RACE CARD
PRICE 1/-
WHIT MONDAY,
MAY 25th,
1931

989
In the presence of Their Royal Highnesses
THE DUKE AND DUCHESS OF YORK
AT BROOKLANDS
GUY'S GALA
JULY 2nd
AND MOTOR RACE DAY
The Autocar
EVERY FRIDAY
4D.
The essential weekly paper for every active motorist—News,
Sport, Road Tests, New Models, Cars and Maintenance,
Tendencies in Car Design and Touring at Home and Abroad.
THE LEADING MOTORING JOURNAL
Published by Iliffe & Sons, Ltd., London, E.C.4

BROOKLANDS
WEYBRIDGE
OFFICIAL
SOUVENIR
PROGRAMME
CAMPBELL TROPHY RACE
1st MAY, 1937
Price - One Shilling
COPYRIGHT.
All literary matter in this Programme,
including the Lists of Competitors, is
Copyright, and any person found making
illegal use thereof will be prosecuted.
THE RIGHT CROWD AND NO CROWDING

THE
INTERNATIONAL
TROPHY
1/- OFFICIAL
PROGRAMME
BROOKLANDS
MONDAY, AUGUST 2nd 1937
START 2-30 P.M. DISTANCE 200 MILES
COPYRIGHT. All literary matter in this Programme, including the Lists of Competitors, is
Copyright, and any person found making illegal use thereof will be prosecuted.
Organised by THE JUNIOR CAR CLUB

THE
INTERNATIONAL
TROPHY
OFFICIAL
PROGRAMME
1/-
BROOKLANDS
MAY 6TH 1933
THE JUNIOR CAR CLUB

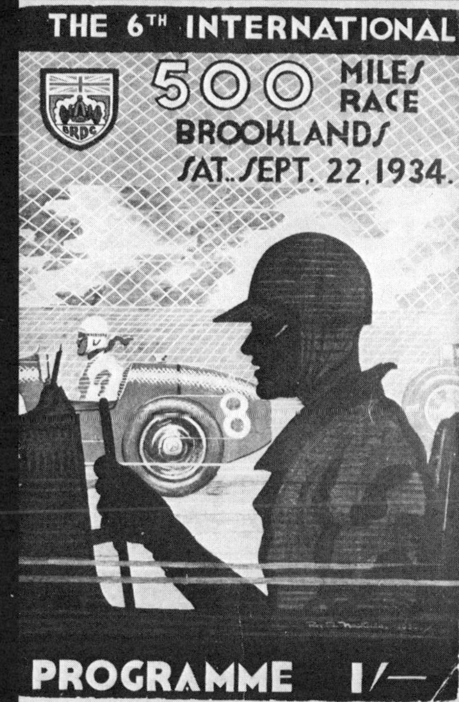

THE 6TH INTERNATIONAL
500 MILES RACE
BROOKLANDS
SAT. SEPT. 22. 1934
8
PROGRAMME 1/-

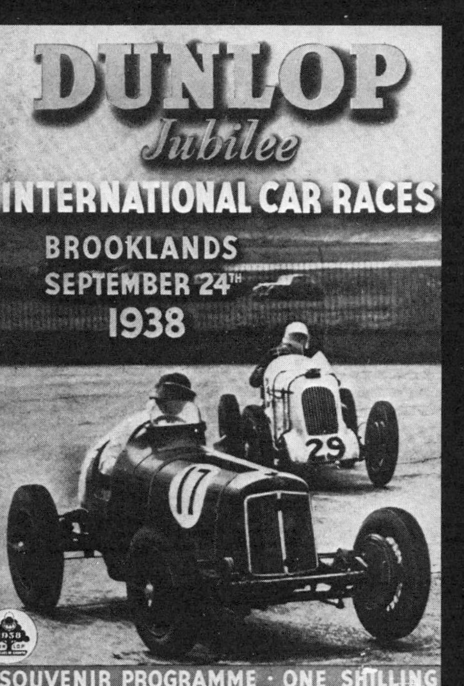

DUNLOP
Jubilee
INTERNATIONAL CAR RACES
BROOKLANDS
SEPTEMBER 24TH
1938
29
7
SOUVENIR PROGRAMME · ONE SHILLING

BROOKLANDS
Saturday MAY 6TH
1939
Light
THE
INTERNATIONAL
TROPHY
Massed start 3 p.m.
OFFICIAL
1/-
PROGRAMME
ORGANISERS: THE JUNIOR CAR CLUB
EMPIRE HOUSE, BROMPTON ROAD, LONDON, S.W.7.

Symbol of the 20th Century
Barrie Pitt, Editor-in-Chief
Ballantine's Illustrated History Books

Few people today would doubt that the car has consolidated its place as the dominant factor in the middle years of the twentieth century.

Its influence pervades almost every aspect of life in the western world, and in the new industrial nations of the east.

Basically, this plain little machine, with an engine to propel it, brakes to slow and stop it, and a wheel to steer it, is a device for moving a small group of people from one place to another. But if that were all, there would be no call for a series such as this. The charm of the car lies in its infinite variety, in the fact that a car is an expression of almost every aspect of human life.

For a few fortunate professional drivers it provides an enjoyable way of earning a living, occasionally the opportunity to make a great deal of money. For many other thousands of young men, rally drivers, kart enthusiasts, drag racers, and amateur racing drivers, it offers a chance to extend their sporting instincts, and in some ways it may be a comparatively harmless substitute for tribal and individual warfare which modern weapons might render all too dangerous.

For others, designers and mechanics, it has provided the opportunity to try their intellectual and creative capacities to the full extent, and thousands of talented people have consequently been liberated by the challenges of automobile design from pedestrian and monotonous occupations to which they might otherwise have been condemned.

But more important than the people who make cars and drive them for sport, in terms of numbers, are the ordinary motorists who buy and use production models, and they too are of an infinite variety. It is probably true to say that in the wealthy societies of the United States and Europe, most people who want to own a car can do so, and they are thereby placed in possession of a device that immediately becomes an extension of their personalities. To some extent indeed, perhaps unjustly, people are judged according to the car they drive, and the car thus becomes a symbol of the man.

Socially, its influence is even more significant, and not entirely beneficial. It crowds our cities, making streets ugly, obstructing efficient street cleaning, destroying the fabric of buildings with its fumes, and killing people in crashes. In motion or stationary, it occupies land on a space-per-car ratio which city real estate values cannot accommodate much longer. And outside towns, roads built to carry the car carve the landscape into sections with no respect for